MOUNTAIN HOUSE

Studies in Elevated Design

Nina Freudenberger

WITH MICHAEL SNYDER

PHOTOGRAPHS BY CHRIS MOTTALINI

 CLARKSON POTTER/PUBLISHERS *New York*

Copyright © 2023 by Nina Freudenberger
Photographs copyright © 2023 by Chris Mottalini

Published in the United States by Clarkson Potter/Publishers, an imprint of the
Crown Publishing Group, a division of Penguin Random House LLC, New York.

ClarksonPotter.com

CLARKSON POTTER is a trademark and POTTER with colophon
is a registered trademark of Penguin Random House LLC.

Library of Congress Cataloging-in-Publication Data
Names: Freudenberger, Nina, author. | Mottalini, Chris, photographer.
Title: Mountain house : studies in elevated design / Nina
    Freudenberger ; photographs by Chris Mottalini.
Description: New York : Clarkson Potter/Publishers, [2023]
Identifiers: LCCN 2022054981 (print) | LCCN 2022054982 (ebook) | ISBN
    9780593233054 (hardcover) | ISBN 9780593233061 (ebook)
Subjects: LCSH: Interior decoration--Themes, motives. | Hillside
    architecture--Themes, motives. | Architecture, Domestic--Themes, motives.
Classification: LCC NK2110 .F675 2023 (print) | LCC NK2110 (ebook) | DDC
    747--dc23/eng/20230412
LC record available at https://lccn.loc.gov/2022054981
LC ebook record available at https://lccn.loc.gov/2022054982

ISBN 978-0-593-23305-4
eISBN 978-0-593-23306-1

Printed in China

Photographer: Chris Mottalini
Writer: Michael Snyder
Editor: Angelin Adams | Editorial assistant: Darian Keels
Designer: Stephanie Huntwork
Production editor: Bridget Sweet
Production manager: Kim Tyner
Compositors: Merri Ann Morrell and Nick Patton
Copy editor: Jenna Dolan | Proofreader: Robin Slutzky
Publicist: Erica Gelbard | Marketer: Andrea Portanova

10 9 8 7 6 5 4 3 2 1

First Edition

For Julian, Wolf & Mike

CONTENTS

FOREWORD

A MOUNTAIN IS OFTEN PRESENTED as an obstacle. If you achieve or complete something difficult, perhaps formerly deemed impossible or foolhardy, we say you "moved mountains" to accomplish it. Or perhaps you worked hard with no results and find yourself, like Sisyphus, the figure of ancient Greek myth, "pushing a boulder up a mountain."

But across literature, film, and music—from religious texts to pop-music standards—there are also visions of mountains as places of romance and wonder, resilience and majesty. To their awe-filled accounts we can now add this collection of exceptional interiors. These mountaintop and mountainside homes, much like mountains themselves, have a beauty that underscores the exertions that made them a reality. The sweat is the point.

If any one thing unites the homes, diverse as they are in style and scale, it's that spirit of persistence in the face of the challenges of a life at high elevations. What happens when we live *with* the elements and the terrain instead of straining to find a way to wrestle them to the ground? Something altogether more interesting—and more magical.

I hope you, like I did, find in this book a new perspective on what it means to design the kind of life you want on your own terms, even against the most demanding and dramatic of backdrops.

—Asad Syrkett

INTRODUCTION

AS AN INTERIOR DESIGNER, I HAVE always been fascinated not only with how people live but also where they choose to live and why. This curiosity brought me to surfing locales around the world in the making of my first book *Surf Shack* and into the most interesting and expansive home libraries in my second book, *Bibliostyle*. As someone who lives in the city and loves to travel with my family, I couldn't help being interested in homes perched in the highest altitudes.

How do we define a mountain house? You might imagine a quaint wooden cottage surrounded by pines, maybe with a stone chimney and billowing smoke, but what I found while working alongside the photographer Chris Mottalini and writer Michael Snyder was just how many ways there are to live with and design for the mountains. A mountain house may not even represent escape to some homeowners—several of the homes we found are primary residences. Some are even located in major world cities.

People have occupied the mountains for just about as long as humans have been around. For nearly 50,000 years, we have had ancestors sheltering under rocks more than 10,000 feet above sea level, and many of our most ancient gods have resided in the mountains. Religious seekers, guerrilla warriors, and political dissidents alike have all treated mountains as retreats from the world, building stupas and monasteries into impossible rockfaces, or establishing alternative societies in the folds of hills where lowland powers can't reach. It's not a coincidence that some of the most biologically, culturally, and linguistically diverse places on earth are mountainous. Mountains seem intimidating, even scary, to those of us who were born and raised at sea level. They remind us of how small we really are, which makes them practically divine.

For the most part the houses included in this book were built, in one way or another, in that ancient tradition of retreat. There are now

A Thinking Man's Chair by Jasper Morrison stands beside a Japanese soaking tub made from reclaimed cedar at Charles de Lisle's Sonoma County cabin.

eight billion people in the world and more than half of us live in cities, which has turned wilderness from something to marvel at or fear into something that many of us yearn for. Some of these houses bring nature close through design choices, such as using organic materials like stone and wood sourced near the homes. Other homeowners quite literally brought the outside in by erecting porous walls or, in some cases, eliminating doors and windows altogether, leaving blank apertures that open to the surrounding landscape. Some of the houses were built with the understanding—radical to city dwellers, logical to everyone else—that everything goes back into the earth. These houses will one day be part of the mountains themselves.

In choosing these homes, we weren't looking for the highest altitudes or the most remote corners of the world, though some are high up and more than a few were hard to get to. Instead, we thought about how architecture and interiors can embody and reflect their surrounding environments. Maybe even more so, we wanted to explore how those environments can, through time, reshape the lives of the people who live within them. Over the course of a year, we traveled to twelve countries on five continents. We met artists and architects, chefs and designers, writers and movie producers. No two people experience their homes in quite the same way, and no two houses are exactly alike. Some are radical, others traditional, some historic and others barely complete. A few are solitary, but most of them were built with family and community in mind. All of them are creative and adaptive and beautiful.

During the pandemic, I found myself, like so many others, yearning for a little space in nature, a little more exterior to explore. More recently—and more resolutely—I've wanted to distance myself from constant accessibility, one of the many downsides to our technology-driven world. These are romantic ideas and still not much easier to manifest in the country than in the city; we had internet access even in the farthest reaches of Patagonia and cell service on a mountaintop in the Austrian Tyrol. But there is something about the sheer fact of distance and the incredible beauty of these landscapes that can put in perspective the endless beeping and buzzing of our devices. In a world this big, nothing is quite so urgent.

CASA RASLEI

DINO PICCOLO AND ALEJANDRA LAUPER

Onsernone Valley, Switzerland

PREVIOUS PAGES: When Piccolo and Lauper first found the house, it was half in ruins. Their intervention involved shoring up the original structure as discreetly as possible.

A paved courtyard with views across the valley to the north-facing slopes preserves the rustic charm of the eighteenth century.

IN 1964, PRECISELY TWO-THIRDS OF the way through his eventful, century-spanning life, Swiss author Max Frisch purchased a modest stone house clinging to a steep Alpine hillside in the village of Berzona. Set deep in the forested folds of the Italian-speaking Swiss canton of Ticino, the Onsernone Valley, where Berzona is located, was a hardscrabble place of tiny granite settlements. Since at least the thirteenth century, when the first written records of settlement in the valley appeared, its residents had survived on farming and husbandry, timber and grain milling, straw weaving, and contraband. In the twentieth century, as the straw trade declined, the valley became popular with German-speaking intellectuals like Max Ernst, pioneer of the Dada and surrealist movements, and, later, Frisch, who used its steep hills and dense fog as the backdrop for his late-career masterpiece *Man in the Holocene*. Published in 1979, the novella follows a lonely retiree (perhaps loosely based on Frisch himself) who spends several days in an unnamed mountain valley contemplating mankind's precarity while cut off from civilization by a landslide. "Nature needs no names," Frisch writes near the novel's end. "The rocks do not need his memory." The valley, in Frisch's rendering, was as alien as it was beautiful, an immortal place not so much lost to time as indifferent to it.

It was through Frisch's writing that, at the age of fifteen, the Zurich-based graphic designer Alejandra Lauper first encountered the Onsernone Valley. "I remember reading him and thinking, 'I have to visit this place,'" she says now. In the early 2000s, Lauper and her husband, Dino Piccolo, came up for summer holidays—Lauper had visited for the first time several years before, in 1994—and rented an eighteenth-century palazzo in Berzona, one of several such mansions built in the eighteenth and nineteenth centuries by locals who'd made small fortunes in Italy and France. Ascending the narrow mountain road that climbs up from

Oxidized steel girders sustain a floating segment of the house's original stacked-stone chimney.

nearby Lake Maggiore, Piccolo remembers village after village appearing around white-knuckle switchbacks, their clock towers rising like bare tree trunks from forests of chestnut, oak, alder and lime. "Spectacular," Piccolo says. "It was love at first sight."

For several years, Piccolo and Lauper and their two young children would return annually to Berzona, forming part of the intellectual community of writers, artists, designers, and architects who had come here for summer retreats since the 1930s. Eventually, they decided to buy land and build a home for themselves. They made their first attempt in Berzona, purchasing an empty plot and commissioning their friend Daniel Buchner, partner in the Basel-based architecture firm Buchner Bründler, to design them a brutalist monolith, "like a giant rock," Piccolo says. After facing staunch resistance from neighbors—in its rigorous minimalism, the house was too modern for local tastes, despite the town's intellectual history—they gave up on building in Berzona. But they never abandoned their dream of a home in Onsernone. Instead, they sought out a pre-existing house where they could realize it more discreetly.

In 2012, a few villages over, they found the ruin they were looking for: a decrepit farmhouse set on seventeen acres, most of which plunged through dense forest down to the glacial waters of the Isorno River. The previous owner, an elderly man, had practically abandoned the house some seven years earlier. On their first visit, Lauper and Piccolo found piles of empty bottles and stacks of old newspapers congealed into blocks as dense and heavy as concrete. After buying the house, they spent two full weeks evacuating eleven tons of debris by helicopter, the only cargo vessel that can enter the valley.

Still, the structure itself was a marvel. The previous owners had preserved the house's twin kitchens—one for summer, on the cool ground floor, and another upstairs for winter, where it soaked in the sparse Alpine sun—and a sagging wooden loggia that connected the three second-floor bedrooms. A wooden grape press languished in a nearby shed, along with tools for peeling back strands of straw to weave into hats and baskets. Entering the house, Lauper says, "you could really feel how they'd lived from the seventeenth century right through to the twentieth."

For the next eighteen months, Lauper, Piccolo, Buchner—who led the design process for the firm—and Bründler developed countless plans for the property. They considered renovating one of the sheds, whose minuscule dimensions more closely resembled the kind of house they'd imagined from the beginning—that is, modest in scale and program—and either razing the main house or leaving it as a ruin. They considered, too, emptying the main house's interior and building an entirely new structure inside, using the half-collapsed stone shell as a protective carapace.

Ultimately, they settled on a set of interventions that barely touched the original structure, as if anything they added might be removed at a moment's notice. Buchner Bründler tore out the house's second floor and installed a massive rectangle of oxidized steel girders, to keep the walls from falling inward and to stabilize the remnants of an original stacked stone fireplace. They filled in the floors with polished concrete, running a channel around the edges to collect the rainwater that, during heavy summer storms, pours in through the open spaces where windows and doors used to be.

The main house's few furnishings—a low bench by a former hearth; a free-floating stair that descends from the main, town-facing entrance, on what had been the second floor; a pair of countertops that, together, depending on

OPPOSITE: A cement-trough bathtub is heated by wood fire and open to the sky through a narrow oculus in the concrete dome overhead.

Wherever possible, the architects left the marks of time visible in the broken plaster of the walls and exposed wooden beams.

the day, function as a kitchen or a sideboard—sprout directly from the floor. "The idea was that we could grow something new from the concrete itself," Piccolo says. More than furniture, these objects resemble abstract sculptures or ancient stone stelae, a perfect encapsulation of Buchner Bründler's approach to design, which Lauper describes as "radically modern but also archaic."

In the former stable, a small annex perpendicular to the house proper, Buchner Bründler built Lauper and Piccolo's primary living space, a single room with a wood-burning stove fitted into the eighteenth-century fireplace, a modest kitchenette, and wooden platforms laid with slender mattresses, where the couple sleeps. Contained within a wooden cube, its interior painted entirely in black, this spartan apartment rests on concrete blocks embedded in the seventy-centimeter-thick stone walls. With its door closed, the room becomes a camera obscura, with three small windows cut deep into the walls. When one steps in from the sun-blasted patio, the room's obliterating darkness comes as a shock, an erasure of the senses that Piccolo describes as "almost an art happening." Eventually, the world outside, glimpsed through those glass lenses, comes into focus, vivid and remote, as if observed through the wrong end of a telescope.

At first glance, the house seems only vaguely habitable, an aesthetic experiment more than an actual home. There is no clearly defined cooking area (though Buchner Bründler left the winter kitchen's sink intact, floating in an upper wall, as witty and useless as a Duchamp readymade). The toilet occupies a plain pine crate below the black-box bedroom, and the only shower is an aluminum tube that runs up an exterior wall, pouring water onto rough granite pavers. A concrete dome punctured by an oculus allows both light and rain to stream down over a bathtub resembling a cement trough, its water warmed by a wood-burning stove. Guests, when they come, sleep on tatami mats laid out by the fireplace or, on warm nights, on the terrace, beneath a sky pixelated with stars.

Porous and provisional, the house demands joyful spontaneity determined less by one's desires than by nature's whims. "If this house had normal, bright rooms or a normal kitchen, it would have become ordinary, but walking down from the village, step by step, you leave the world behind—and you have that experience every time," Piccolo says. "To be here, you have to change the way you live, the way you think, your whole way of being."

Yet, for all its severity, the house is also surprisingly pleasant and homely. The elements are not a hardship here. They're a material as essential as concrete or stone or steel. "We weren't looking for the comforts we have in Zurich," Lauper says. "Even just where the house stands, one hundred meters down from the street, makes it impossible to have a normal, modern life." Instead, Piccolo and Lauper come here, in part, for the pleasures of work: cultivating grapes, mowing the grass, maintaining the stone walls, or splitting wood. When the day's work ends, they read or hike, chasing the receding sun up the hillside that connects the house to the village. They forage for mushrooms, eat simple food cooked wherever they like, and swim in the river—clear and cool as crystal—drying themselves like lizards on sunbaked rocks worn smooth by the water. These pleasures, like nature itself, need no names. The stones have memories of their own.

Interventions in the main house by Buchner Bründler consist mostly of freestanding objects that seem to grow out of the polished concrete floor, like the staircase pictured here.

OPPOSITE: The architects developed and discarded several plans for the house, including one that involved leaving the main house in ruins and adapting a nearby shed, pictured here, for habitation.

A view over the San Gabriel Mountains outside
Los Angeles.

SAN GABRIEL
MOUNTAIN CABIN

ANN AND ANTHONY RUSSO
Big Santa Anita Canyon, California

WHEN COOL AIR ROLLS EAST OFF THE Pacific and over the Los Angeles Basin, the first high peaks it reaches are the front range of the San Gabriel Mountains, rising an average of five thousand feet above the low-lying sprawl of Los Angeles. As the air rises, it drops precipitation over the mountain face—more than thirty inches a year compared with about a foot in the city—birthing rivers and streams like those in the Big Santa Anita Canyon that irrigate forests of sixty-foot alders and incense cedars, canyon live oak and bigcone firs.

Beginning in 1907, the newly formed US Forest Service—it was founded in 1905—opened swaths of the San Gabriels to private development, hoping that allowing some settlement in the area would turn casual visitors into citizen conservators. They hoped, too, that by assigning lots, they might control previously unchecked development while creating a local economy. During Prohibition, the cabins in the Big Santa Anita Canyon sat off the legal grid; according to local lore, residents maintained clandestine stills and brothels and threw wild weekend parties. By the mid-1930s, there were thousands of cabins scattered through the San Gabriels, most of which were destroyed by a succession of floods and fires—most recently, the Bobcat Fire of 2020. Having consumed seventeen of the remaining cabins in the canyon, the Bobcat reduced the total number there to just sixty-three, one of which—a modest wooden structure built on stone foundations pulled directly out of the creek below—belongs to Ann and Anthony Russo.

Anthony Russo, a producer and director in Hollywood, lives full time with his family in Pasadena, on the northeastern side of greater LA, but both he and his wife grew up in eastern cities (Ann in New York, Anthony in Cleveland). Filled with deciduous greenery, those cities are a far cry from LA's sepia sunshine and spindly palms. "My wife and I have lived in Los Angeles for twenty years or so, and from the beginning, the

San Gabriels were our favorite getaway. You're just transported to an environment that feels a lot more familiar," Anthony says. "The idea that you can start in Los Angeles, in a semi-desert, and then climb several thousand feet and, all of a sudden, be in an environment that feels completely different—that's very powerful to me."

For several years, the Russos kept an eye on real estate listings in the canyon, but the Forest Service cabins go up for sale rarely, and the program for building new ones ended in 1936. The property Ann and Anthony ended up buying, built on a steep slope rising straight out of the creek, had been in the previous owners' family for decades; it was the family before *them* that built the three-hundred-gallon cistern that draws on the creek to provide the cabin with water throughout the year.

Much remains the same today as it was then. To arrive at the cabin, the Russos climb two thousand feet into the mountains on switchback roads, a thirty-minute drive from their front door that ends in a one-mile walk down to the cabin. The only energy sources are a fireplace, propane tanks (brought in by pack mules) that run the refrigerator and the stove, and solar panels used for charging eight Absorbent Glass Mat car batteries, a more recent technology. The only communication is a century-old crank phone, part of one of the oldest functioning telephone systems in the United States, which connects the cabins to a still-operating donkey pack station and, in case of emergency, to one another. "You're very dependent on your neighbors and community," Anthony says, "so that's fun and charming and invigorating, this need for one another on a practical level." For Russo, this sense of isolation, combined with the remarkable nearness to his family's primary home, is an important part of the cabin's magic.

With roughly seven hundred square feet of interior space, the cabin almost imitates the tight, angular proportions of the canyon itself, with its steep mountain walls and the cascading stream where the Russos' children have spent afternoons scrambling over boulders. (The family's visits to the cabin have been restricted since the September 2020 fire.) At the center of the house, a river stone fireplace is "the place where the house meets the landscape," Anthony says. In the afternoons, light pours in from windows installed high on the nearly double-height walls, directing your gaze up past the steep canyon and toward a patch of virgin sky.

Throughout the house—its interiors were remodeled by LA-based firm Commune Design—the spaces are modest and tightly packed, as though the walls themselves were huddling around the fireplace for protection against an evening chill. Materials throughout the cabin—with the exception of the stones pulled from the creek bed—were carried to the building site either by pack mule or by hand including the white-oak cabinet fronts used for the efficient, functional kitchen and the grass cloth ceiling panels in the lofted bedroom, meditative and warm as a Japanese tearoom. Electrical wiring that runs, exposed, over the surfaces of the lime-washed stone walls speaks to a present that sits lightly atop the past. Anthony recalls the first night he and his kids stayed overnight in the cabin, which was completed in September 2021. He was lying in the sleeping loft with his son: "The windows were open, and we were just listening to the creek," he says. "I remember it felt very powerful . . . knowing that my son was probably having a very similar experience. I remember the peacefulness of that."

This kind of communion is what these houses (and the National Park Service more broadly) were designed for—not just communion with nature, but communion with one another, which, ultimately, are one and the same.

OPPOSITE: A wooden ladder ascends from the kitchen and breakfast nook to the sleeping loft upstairs.

An original crank phone connects the cabin to a (still operational) donkey station and the other cabins in the valley.

Grass cloth ceiling panels in the lofted bedroom recall shoji panels in a Japanese tearoom.

Water for the shower shed, a separate structure from the cabin and outhouse, comes from a 300-gallon cistern filled from the creek below.

OPPOSITE: The final arrival to the cabin involves a one-mile hike down from the nearest parking spot.

AFRA HOUSE

MICHEL PIQUEMAL
High Atlas, Morocco

Simple meals of homemade tagine are taken on the back terrace with views over the rugged High Atlas.

NEXT PAGES: An accumulation of textiles lends warmth to a casual sitting room.

THE LANDSCAPE ARCHITECT ERIC Ossart was twenty-one years old the first time he crossed the High Atlas, the spine of mountains that separates Morocco's Atlantic coast from the Sahara. Born in France, Ossart had moved with his family to Morocco in 1960 at just two weeks old, the year before the Bouknadel Gardens, located a short distance northeast of Rabat, the nation's capital, opened to the public. From an early age, Ossart would visit the gardens with his family, and by age twelve, he knew he wanted to create spaces as richly textured and alive as these. Six years later, he moved to France to pursue his degree at the National School of Landscape Architecture, in Versailles, but no place captured his imagination quite like the rugged escarpments and snowcapped peaks of the Atlas.

In the early 2000s, Ossart and his partner, Arnaud Maurières—they met as students at Versailles—settled in the walled city of Taroudant in southwestern Morocco. As they studied

and specialized in the traditional earthen construction of the region—a mix of adobe and compacted earth—Ossart and Maurières would take weekend trips into the mountains, traversing sheltered valleys as they passed from village to village, much as Ossart had done in his youth. On one of those trips, in 2004, they came across a traditional earthen house set high on a terraced hillside outside the village of Imoulass. "The house was in ruins, falling to the ground," Ossart says, but the foundations were strong, and the vistas over the hills and valleys—planted with eggplant and tomato, olive and argan trees—were spectacular.

The find was also serendipitous. Not long before, Ossart and Maurières had met the French children's book writer Michel Piquemal through mutual friends. Sometime later, they showed Piquemal images of the house, telling him they were hesitant to buy it themselves, as they already had projects under way. Piquemal agreed to purchase the house, but only on the

condition that they and their team handle the restoration. The collaboration seemed almost predestined.

Over the next three years, they rebuilt the house and its gardens piece by piece, excavating four terraces from the hillside, using the clay-rich earth to rebuild the walls and the extracted stones to weave pathways through what would soon be the house's gardens. At the time, there was no electricity, the only connection between Taroudant and Imoulass was a rough dirt road, and the only means of transporting building materials to the house was via the village's two donkeys. "It was really important to me to work with local materials, local techniques, and local people," says Piquemal; the house's isolation ensured that there would be no other way. The final result, he says, is both "austere" and "almost pharaonic," the house's lime-slaked, rectangular volumes looking out from its bluff like a temple. Inside, Ossart says, the house obeys the traditional logic of what was once a nomadic society, its furnishings (trunks and tapestries and niches filled with books) consisting of little that can't be packed up and moved.

For at least the first year in the house, Piquemal and his family lived by candlelight, bathing themselves in the hammam-style bathroom Ossart and Maurières had designed using a traditional wood-burning oven to heat both the water and the floors. "I remember that when my daughter was a little girl, every time we came from France, she was amazed by the fact that we could live like that and life went on," Piquemal recalls. By day, the family would go for long walks in the valley or take shelter from the highland sun behind walls nearly twenty inches thick and punctured with windows that threw beams of light across the terra-cotta floors.

Over the years, Ossart and Maurières's desert garden has grown in slowly but magnificently, using what minimal water can be accumulated from the communal irrigation system to which the house has access for just one hour three times a month. Yuccas and agaves that Ossart and Maurières brought in from their home, in central Mexico, now thrive alongside euphorbias from Madagascar and native blue fan palms. It is a botanical garden in miniature, an arid iteration of the Bouknadel, where Ossart spent his childhood.

"The house was built the same way it would have been a century before," Ossart says, "and it's a good thing we built it when we did, because it was the end of an era." Some years after the house's completion in 2007, pavement and electricity entered the valley, and the traditional skills that made it possible to restore the house using the original construction techniques began to disappear. Still, he says, the rhythm of life in the valley remains similar, with its agricultural cycles and Sunday markets. Also, the shared taxis that connect the village to the city, twenty miles away, make visiting the house an easier drive now—but, still, it's a journey. "As soon as I arrive, I slow down," Piquemal says. "Your brain changes. You can see life happening, you see people cultivating crops and talking. You can spend hours just looking at the landscape or contemplating the sky."

However many things have changed, that sky remains unaltered, as much a source of inspiration for Piquemal as it is for the artists and writers to whom he has lent the house, to spark their own reveries. "We have the most beautiful sky here—or, in any case, more beautiful than the sky in France," he says. Studded with stars and clear as crystal, it's a sky that demands nothing beyond the silent observation of time as it passes. "Western life," Piquemal says, "has robbed us of that light."

Wooden slats cast shadows on the mud walls of the
dim entry hall, a reprieve from the harsh mountain sun.

Rustic wooden columns line the gallery on the house's second floor with views down to the interior courtyard.

A sink in the courtyard outside the bedrooms stands
alongside the opening to a wood-burning oven used to
heat water for the shower.

OPPOSITE: Over the years, the gardens have grown in
with species both local and exotic, brought in from as
far afield as Mexico and Madagascar.

OPPOSITE: The house's thick adobe walls keep the kitchen, pictured here with its shelves of traditional cooking implements, cool even at the height of summer.

Meticulous notes track the planting and progress of the house's desert garden.

The guest bedroom on the ground floor exemplifies the house's humble design, with the mattress laid out on a stone plinth.

A valley in Morocco's High Atlas Mountains.

VILL'ALCINA

SERGIO FERNANDEZ
Caminha, Portugal

IN AUGUST 1974, ARCHITECT SERGIO Fernandez stayed for the first time in the week-end house he'd built for himself on a forested bluff over the Minho River, which separates Portugal from Galicia, in northwestern Spain. Before breaking ground on the house, Fernandez had used the land—a long, narrow plot above the medieval village of Caminha—to host political meetings disguised as picnics at which he and his friends could openly denounce the authoritarian regime that had controlled their country since 1933.

In those days, he recalls, "we couldn't speak freely anywhere; there were police all over." Sheltered from harsh winds by Monte Santa Tecla, rising across the water, this place became, if briefly, one of safety and dissidence, an idyllic refuge from surveillance and spies. Then, in April 1974, the bloodless Carnation Revolution brought the dictatorship to an end. Fernandez's first holidays in his cliffside villa became a celebration of Portugal's suddenly

wide-open future. The house, in its own small way, was, too.

Like many right-wing despots, the founder of the Portuguese dictatorship, António de Oliveira Salazar, used architecture as a tool for projecting state power—in part through nostalgia for rural aesthetics and ornament. As part of his nationalist fantasy, Salazar hoped, in particular, to develop a model vision for a traditional Portuguese home.

At the other end of the political spectrum, radical young designers replicated the modernist experiments of masters like Le Corbusier and Mies van der Rohe, but eventually grew dissatisfied with their derivative explorations. In 1955, a group of eighteen architects initiated a national survey on vernacular architecture funded by the state. In the introduction to the survey, published in 1961, the authors—most prominently Fernandez's teacher Fernando Távora—declared, "There is no existing 'Portuguese Architecture' or a typical Portuguese

house." The domestic architecture they proposed would not necessarily *look* traditional, but would instead adapt the rigorous abstractions of modernity to a modest scale and materiality incorporating, they wrote, the "lessons of coherence, honesty, economy, skill, function and beauty" that traditional architecture might impart. Modernity, with all its optimistic and forward-looking implications, would be a continuation of the past rather than a rupture.

Though Fernandez did not participate in the survey himself, he studied under Távora during the years of its creation, and its findings deeply influenced his future work. The house outside Caminha—really, a pair of identical houses connected by a carport, one for him and one for a friend with whom he'd purchased the property—emerged directly from that quiet rebellion. In 1963, two years after the survey's publication, Fernandez moved for a year to the remote inland village of Rio de Onor, far removed from the comforts of Porto, the seaside city where he'd been raised. The village had neither water nor electricity. In the winter, snow blew through empty window frames. Until then, Fernandez and his entire circle, including his close friend Álvaro Siza, future winner of the prestigious Pritzker Architecture Prize, "all lived in big towns. Portugal was something we'd forgotten," he says. "We had no relationship with it."

That year in Rio de Onor "was the most important experience of my life as an architect," Fernandez says now, some sixty years later, despite the fact that he never completed a project there. "It was how I learned to pay profound attention to what people used and needed. It brought me closer to reality." In that brief time in his country's hinterlands, Fernandez developed a clear set of values for his future architecture, values similar to those outlined in the survey: "economy, simplicity, the sense of not being an

exhibitionist, of being common," as he puts it now, "and of being comfortable, if possible."

The house in Caminha exemplifies that austere warmth. Built from local granite and rough concrete now sheathed in a ruffled slip of creeping fig, the 1,186-square-foot house descends over its hillside in three half floors set into the rock like agricultural terraces. Almost invisible among the trees, the house recalls the schist villages that crown hilltops across central Portugal like graphite-gray crests on waves of eucalyptus and pine.

The front door, tucked around the eastern side of the house, opens onto a landing that drops immediately into a brief flight of stairs flanked on one side by cedar cabinets, their tops crowded with objects Fernandez has collected through decades of travel in Europe, Africa, Asia, and the Americas. Model boats and pottery share the space with a salvaged threshing board, its timeworn surface washed with sunshine from a skylight just overhead, and with a grinning sculpture by a local artist, meant, Fernandez says, to represent a legendary medieval king but dressed anachronistically in the military uniform of the Salazar years.

That stair leads down to a narrow hall that runs from a utilitarian kitchen at one end to Fernandez's bedroom at the other. Opening off the corridor, two guest bedrooms occupy a pair of meditative cells with futons and sage-green curtains that zip up for privacy or open onto picture windows with expansive views across the river to Spain.

Panels of West African *tola* wood line the sloped ceiling like the hull of a sailboat. The builder who worked on the house with Fernandez had previously made a living building pleasure boats for rich clients in Lisbon. (Fernandez, for his part, has never sailed: "Me and water, we're not friendly," he says.) Though the house's

Soot stones on the modest hearth in the house's living room have accumulated over nearly fifty years of frequent use.

Cubby-like guest rooms are enclosed behind zippered curtains that open onto panoramic views of Monte Santa Tecla on the Spanish side of the Minho.

interior layout is as clear and rational as the rigid glass boxes of mid-century America, the materials throughout are tactile and alive—rough stone, cement, and wood; sun-bleached kilims and cotton slipcovers in mineral shades of ochre, sienna, and cobalt.

On the house's lowest tier, the living room centers on a soot-stained hearth flanked by bookshelves and stacked wood, dinged-up weights for fishing nets, and baskets of pine-cones Fernandez collected from the surrounding wood. Even a pair of severe LC2s—the iconic chair of tubular steel frames and boxy leather cushions designed in 1928 by Le Corbusier, Pierre Jeanneret, and Charlotte Perriand—are softened here with pale lavender upholstery and a cream-colored powder coat on the metal. Outside, the forest gathers close, allowing only brief glimpses of the landscape beyond.

Solitary but never lonely, the house reads from some angles as a harsh brutalist mass and from others as an outgrowth of the mountainside, a masterpiece of mid-century logic and a simple village home. At the time of its design, this combination of tradition and modernity made it a private act of dissent. "The idea," Fernandez says, "was for the house to be nothing more than a stone wall, just like the face of the mountain—no more than this."

But a stone wall is itself far more than a structure. It belongs neither to the past nor to the future. It can be a shelter from the elements and from prying eyes, a historic relic and a modern monolith. In building something new, Fernandez also built something timeless: the echo of a rural world quickly disappearing and the foundation for a life well lived.

Faded kilims, gathered on Fernandez's travels, line the narrow hallway that connects his bedroom to the house's common areas.

The structure of granite and concrete is now overgrown with a fine mesh of creeping fig.

A hillside chapel in the interior mountains of northern Portugal.

DREAM HOUSE

BRIAN PERSICO AND HANNAH HAWORTH
Windham, New York

PREVIOUS PAGES: Built on a footprint of less than 550 square feet, the structure almost resembles an urban townhouse in its tall, narrow proportions.

Whimsical Josef Frank wallpaper in the primary bedroom, originally designed in the 1940s at the height of modernism, evokes the same playful indifference to contemporary fashion as Persico's furniture.

NEXT PAGES: Persico crafted the kitchen cabinets using solid timber originally felled to make room for the septic field and later recycled for benches for the couple's wedding at the house.

FOR YEARS, FURNITURE DESIGNER Brian Persico has had a recurring dream about the two-hundred-square-foot family cabin in the Catskills where he spent weekends as a kid. In that dream, he opens a familiar door into a room he's never seen before. Moving forward, he steps from one phantom room to another, inventing spaces with every step, a literal dream house materializing out of his imagination. The experience, he says, is joyful and surreal and "overwhelmingly nostalgic"—memory reconfigured into something surprising and new.

The cabin in Windham, New York, has been in Persico's family since the 1970s, when his father built it on a wooded patch of land he'd purchased among the undulant hills of Upstate New York. Every other weekend throughout his childhood, Persico's family visited the house, skiing at nearby Windham Mountain in winter and playing in the surrounding woods in summer. "I was so obsessed as a child, I always wanted to live there," Persico says. "It was just a really magical place."

As he grew up, the experience of staying in the house, which had electricity but no water, became less appealing to his parents, who preferred the comforts of a nearby bed-and-breakfast. Persico became the unofficial caretaker of their no-frills lodge and, beginning in high school, started throwing raucous parties out in the woods, a tradition that continued through college and into his twenties, as he established himself as a designer in New York City. It was at one of these parties in 2013 that he met his wife, Hannah Haworth, who worked at the time for the design studio BDDW. A week later, and virtually every weekend after that, he and Haworth returned to the cabin as a couple.

Within a year, Haworth and Persico had moved into an apartment together in Red Hook, Brooklyn and, within two years, Haworth had decided to leave her job at BDDW. She wanted to focus instead on a small business she'd started importing hand-woven fabrics from around the world, beginning with indigo-dyed cottons

woven by childhood friends from the Mangyan peoples of Mindoro Island in the Philippines, where she'd grown up. Persico already ran his own small business, which meant the two had nothing tying them to the city. They decided to move to Windham full time.

Initially, they'd planned simply to expand the cabin, which was as charged with the memories of their first years together as it was with Persico's family history. "But the idea of changing something that was so special, cutting it up and altering it, seemed sacrilegious," Persico says. The choice to preserve the cabin as it was, Haworth continues, "freed us up to create something for our new life together rather than trying to implant something in the cabin." In 2016, they moved the cabin about two hundred feet from its original site to free up the best parcel of hilltop land. The following year, they started to build.

The design for the house came together spontaneously, shaped as much by the vernacular style of the Catskills as by the couple's tight budget. Working with friends and family—including a close family friend of Persico's who had years of experience in timber framing and Haworth's brother, similarly experienced in stick framing—they erected a sturdy pine skeleton and covered it with whitewashed clapboard. Set on a slender footprint of five hundred square feet, the house rises two and a half stories into the woods, its tall, narrow form both awkward and whimsical, like something out of a Roald Dahl story. "You can tell we lived in the city; we basically built a townhouse," Persico says. Haworth laughs: "And then we put the door on the wrong way."

Since then, the house has taken on color and texture and memories as rich as those embedded in the original cabin, which, now outfitted with running water, serves as a guesthouse. In 2017, Persico and Haworth got married on the property, building rustic benches for their guests from an acre of trees they'd felled for the obligatory septic field. When Haworth became pregnant the following year, they decided the time had come to build a proper kitchen to replace their hot plate and basement pantry. Persico put the wedding bench lumber to use again, making the cabinet frames from sturdy maple and the doors from pine, which they painted white. Haworth gave birth in 2019, and their daughter would go on to learn her first words—among them, *bird* and *fish*—from hours spent crawling around after chickens and absorbed by the koi ponds and fruit trees depicted in the playful Josef Frank wallpaper hung in her parents' bedroom. Haworth gave birth to their second child, a boy, at home.

Distance from the city and proximity to nature have enriched both Persico's and Haworth's work. Despite its modest size, the house gave Haworth the space to accumulate textiles imported from India, Guatemala, the Philippines, and Scotland, where she was born. Persico, meanwhile, now has better access than ever to the ancestral crafts and techniques that inform his furniture designs, whose delicate proportions and impeccable construction gesture toward honest Shaker functionality. Deep in the woods, they have left behind New York's competitive and, ultimately, rigid design scene. "We're not looking over our shoulder anymore to see what other people are making," Haworth says.

Their respective skill sets, combined with a shared creative drive and fascination with natural materials, have allowed Persico and Haworth to transform the house by hand, turning every square inch into a space for experimentation and self-expression. Bedspreads and upholstery throughout the house come from Haworth's collection of Kutchi wools and cottons from the deserts of northwest India, while the duvet covers are stuffed with downy milkweed seedpods that she and her daughter collect each year in the waning days of summer. Save for a single BDDW lamp in the living room, Persico crafted every piece of furniture in the house, from those kitchen cabinets, now washed in a rich bottle green chosen by Haworth—"She's way more fearless with color than I am," Persico says—to the rotating collection of chairs around the kitchen table. The joyful brutality of a young family makes for ideal quality control, the sturdy grace of stamina a better metric for design than the prevailing trends of any given moment.

As in Persico's recurring dream, the Windham house will continue to grow and change. Soon, Persico will start work on a studio for himself on the property—for now, he rents in a nearby town—and, eventually, on a freestanding space for Haworth as well. They want to re-shingle the roof with cedar or slate and maybe replace the iron stovepipe that bends up and out of the living room with a brick fireplace. They have big plans, a future still to build; some of it is carefully conceived, much of it is roughly sketched. "You have these dreams, and they end up being a reason to live. Accomplishing them isn't even necessarily part of it," Persico says. "Sometimes you just need to make something."

The interior of Persico and Haworth's sugar shack, where they process the sap tapped from maple trees on the property; the space also doubles as a toolshed.

OPPOSITE: Persico timber-framed the sugar shack himself, initially with the intention of using it as a chicken coop.

An Alpine valley seen from a quiet perch above the
Austrian village of Mayrhofen.

TYROLEAN OUTPOST

MARIELLA AND RUTGER VAN DER ZEE
Mayrhofen, Austria

THE LEGEND OF MARIELLA VAN DER Zee's family cabin in the Austrian Alps begins with a countess and a bear.

Around the turn of the twentieth century, when the Tyrol was still under Hapsburg control, one of van der Zee's forefathers worked as a gamekeeper for absentee aristocrats who, prior to World War I, came to the Ziller Valley (or Zillertal), in what is now Western Austria, to hunt. On one of the count's visits, the story has it, van der Zee's great-great-great-grandfather—Mariella is not sure how many generations ago this was—fended off an ursine assailant, winning the nobleman's gratitude and, with it, a simple wooden hunting cabin that he had built for the count years earlier. Perched on a 6,500-foot peak overlooking the village of Mayrhofen, where van der Zee (née Kröll) grew up, the cabin has been in the family ever since.

By the early 1900s, alpinism had been a popular pastime for European elites for half a century, with the Zillertal as one of its focal points. But for locals like van der Zee's forebears, who worked as farmers and mountain guides, holidays "didn't really exist," she says. In the early years of their stewardship, van der Zee's predecessors would hole up in the cabin for multi-day hunting trips, stopping along the way to collect wild chanterelles or blueberries. Each night, they would flash their lanterns in an "All's well" sign to their wives and children in the valley; if an emergency arose, the families would lay out white sheets on their lawns, clearly visible from the peak, to indicate that the men were needed back.

By the time of van der Zee's childhood in the early '90s, Mayrhofen had been transformed into a resort town for skiers and hikers. Van der Zee herself climbed to the cabin for the first time around the age of eight, accompanying her mother (an avid climber), one of her mother's close friends, and that friend's son. "I remember it was really magical," she recalls. "You could play all day, picking flowers

and berries and looking for ruined cabins in the woods." There was also, she says, "an element of danger." On that first climb, van der Zee remembers watching the steady advance of afternoon thunderheads, which unleashed a squall overhead as evening fell. "I remember it felt really exciting but also a bit unsafe, and I think that adds to the magic," she says now. "The mountain is boss. It's Nature's country."

That experience repeated itself nearly two decades later, when van der Zee came to the cabin for the first time with her future husband, Rutger, whose careers have included graphic designer, line cook, filmmaker, movement coach, and, most recently, furniture designer and woodworker. The couple met in Mayrhofen around 2007. Rutger, who grew up in Amsterdam, had come to the valley to make snowboarding films, while Mariella, who moved to London at eighteen to work in fashion, had returned there for vacation. Before long, Rutger had relocated to the United Kingdom to pursue both his new Austrian girlfriend and a career in film.

Eventually, the couple started to fantasize about the countryside. "Both of our best childhood memories have to do with independence, with staying out until the street lights go off," Rutger says. For Mariella, excitement no longer compensated for the anxieties of urban anonymity. "You start to long for what you had when you were younger," she says. And so, in the summer of 2018, after a five-year stint in Amsterdam, the couple moved to Mayrhofen, where they had their oldest son and, shortly after, married. Once in Austria, Rutger trained for the title of master cabinetmaker and has since opened his own workshop, called Studio van der Zee, focused on bold, sculptural furniture. Mariella works as a freelance photographer and art director.

The valley, like anyplace else, has changed, Mariella says, but the trail to the cabin—used by members of her family and by the hunters who stay at the only other cabin on the route—has not. The hike begins at a cable bridge over a narrow river. On the other side, a path winds through dense woods before opening onto a meadow of dew-slick grass. Where the meadow ends, the trail climbs through stands of spruce, fir, and stone pine, growing narrower and steeper as it progresses. It can take as long as four hours (or as few as two, Rutger says) to pass the tree line where the cabin materializes among blossoms of maidenstears and arnica and tufted seed heads of pasqueflowers past their bloom.

Little more than a wooden crate constructed from hand-sawed beams, the cabin has just one interior room, with a small wooden table, a stove top, and cushions that serve as a sleeping cot. A handful of family photos on the back wall are the only objects that might count as decorative. There is no electricity, and potable water comes from a mountain spring a fifteen-minute walk away along a narrow path cinched around the western edge of the slope. A haphazard porch looks out over three valleys threaded between steep slopes quilted with pastureland and forest.

Even in her childhood, Mariella rarely made this climb more than twice a year, deterred by inclement weather and difficulty. Since she and Rutger started a family, her visits have become even less frequent. Rutger goes a couple of times each year with friends, but never for more than a night. The two sometimes talk about building out the cabin's interior with Rutger's meticulous carpentry, so they might consider longer stays once their children are old enough. For now, distance remains part of the cabin's allure. "The mountain doesn't give you anything for free. You have to earn every single meter," Mariella says. "The fact that you have to work hard for it makes it mean so much more."

A family memorial attached to the cabin was carved in honor of Mariella's great uncle but has since come to stand for all loved ones lost.

Perched nearly 4,000 feet above the ski town of
Mayrhofen, the lodge commands spectacular views
of three interlinked valleys.

CONCRETE BOX HOUSE AND EARTH HOUSE

BYOUNG CHO AND ENSIL KIM
Yangpyeong, South Korea

IN THE AUTUMN OF 2004, ARCHITECT Byoung Cho made a visit to what was then the construction site of his country house in the hilly district of Yangpyeong, some thirty miles east of central Seoul. The house, at that point, consisted of raw concrete walls, a concrete roof, centuries-old wooden columns that Cho had recovered from a pair of demolished Buddhist temples, and a twenty-four-foot-square court-yard that opened upward to a bare patch of sky. "I walked in, and I was amazed at how beautiful it was," he recalls now, twenty years later. "It was like an abandoned temple in the deep mountains." When he returned to the finished project later that year, the walls had been painted a pristine white, the floors covered in slick pine. The temple had become the house he would visit almost every weekend he spent in his native South Korea. The house in its completed form "was so disappointing," Cho says with a self-deprecating laugh and a shrug. "I always missed that first moment."

Cho started his Seoul-based firm BCHO Architects a little under a decade before building the country house and had spent those early years on projects that conformed to the desires and tastes of his clients rather than to his own interests and preoccupations. One of those houses, also in Yangpyeong, had generated considerable interest among the client's friends, many of them artists. After seeing Cho's work, they encouraged the client to find a piece of land they could all invest in and build on together, to create a self-contained artists' village that Cho would design. Before long, the client, along with twenty-five investors, had bought thirty acres of land. In exchange for laying out road access and property lines on the hilly site, and for designing or approving all future construction, the investors offered Cho the central plot.

"Of course, I didn't have any money, and I needed to build the cheapest house I could," Cho says. "At the time, my office built everything

we designed, so I asked my construction team what materials we had on hand, and they told me we had cement and three-point-six-meter wooden forms. I said, 'Okay, so that's the building height: three-point-six meters'"—roughly twelve feet. To further reduce costs, Cho used the recycled columns, which he'd held in storage for several years. He conceived of the house's simple form in order to build with just two pours of concrete, one for the foundations and the floor, another for the walls and roof; typically, Cho says, his houses can't be done with fewer than seven pours.

"For me, the house was an experiment in minimum architectural intervention to allow for the maximum experience of the earth, trees, water, sky," he says. By his standards, though, the experiment did not go far enough. Initially, he had wanted to bury the house entirely, a realization of his long-standing interest in an architecture "that offered *only* experience, that had no form at all," he says. These ideas had occupied his attention since his time as a graduate student at Harvard, where his thesis project drew connections between ancient Taoist ideas about negative and positive space (*un* and *yen* in Korean philosophy) and the early works of American artist Richard Serra, particularly his *House of Cards*, which balanced four lead slabs in the form of a box. How, Cho asked, could architecture explore what was *not there*, the *un* of built space rather than the *yen*?

Cho's team and his contractors objected to these plans, citing (not unreasonably) the potential problems with humidity and ventilation. He acquiesced and, rather than embedding the house in its hillside, set it down on its gently sloped plot, organizing it around the ordinary spaces one needs to live—a kitchen, a bedroom, a bathroom—and a courtyard water garden for passing slow days under a canopy of trees that changed with the seasons.

When Cho's brother, one of the original investors in the artists' village, decided to sell his own lot in 2008, Cho purchased the land and took the opportunity to "build the house the *right* way," he says. Digging a 350-square-foot pit, he poured a slender concrete retaining wall and used the excavated soil to make rammed earth walls. Afterward, he poured a concrete roof over half the space, leaving the other half open to the elements. Inside, he used rice paper walls and floors made of *hanji* (a tough mulberry bark parchment cured with soy oil) to lend the space the snug intimacy of an old *hanok*, Korea's traditional courtyard houses. "The idea was that, someday, when we no longer need it, the house could just disappear into the earth," Cho says. "We could demolish the shell, hopefully reuse the concrete, but the earth would just go back into the ground." He called the project the Earth House.

Whereas the Concrete Box functioned as a conventional home, the Earth House was conceived as a space of ritual and meditation, dedicated to poetry and conversation and somber celebration. At the Concrete Box house, Cho and his wife, Ensil Kim, would invite friends for barbecues and small gatherings; at the Earth House—which, at night, glows like a subterranean beacon—they focused on more contemplative pleasures. "I decided to make my own temple," Cho says, dedicating the house to Korean poet Yoon Dong-ju, who died in a Japanese prison in 1945 at age twenty-seven, mere months before Korea's liberation from Japan's thirty-five-year occupation. Cho returns regularly to Yoon's work, as austere in its beauty as his buildings, and to one poem in particular, called "Self-Portrait":

OPPOSITE: Built four years after the Concrete Box House, Cho's Earth House, set on a neighboring plot, is entirely embedded in the ground, an exploration of architecture not as an object but as pure experience.

Designed to be simple and cost-effective, Concrete Box House was built with just two pours of concrete as compared with a minimum of seven for most of Cho's projects.

"All alone I visit a deserted well by a paddy-field beyond the hill / Then I quietly look in the water," the poem begins. Yoon, as narrator, describes his comings and goings from the well, his vacillation between hatred and mercy for the man he sees reflected there and his compulsion to return to his own reflection. "In the well the moon is bright; clouds saunter, the sky spreads; the blue winds breathe;" he writes, drawing his meditation on frailty and compassion to a close. "The autumn dwells; and the man stands there like a memory."

Like Yoon returning to his well, Cho returned to his Concrete Box house countless times, despite that initial disappointment. Then, in 2021, while making repairs to the windows that open onto the courtyard, he decided to rip out the house's refined interiors, returning it to the condition that had enchanted him twenty years before. Today, the concrete walls are exposed. The ground is gravel. The Concrete Box is, once again, an abandoned temple deep in the mountains, a meditative extension of the Earth House sunk like a well into the hill below. Cho rarely sleeps here now, using the property instead as a place to gather friends and colleagues, who come for daylong retreats spent cleaning autumn leaves from the surface of the water garden, drinking tea and wine, and talking about the ideas of *mak* and *bium* (imperfection and emptiness) that shape the aesthetic sensibility of their rugged homeland.

Half-destroyed, the house now stands poised between oblivion and rebirth, darkness and light, *un* and *yen*. Both the Concrete Box and the Earth House will eventually disappear, as all things do; in their grandeur and indifference, mountains may be the world's clearest reminder of this humbling truth. When that happens, they will leave behind the bright moon, the sauntering clouds, the spreading sky, the blue wind. The people who once stood there will be nothing more than a memory.

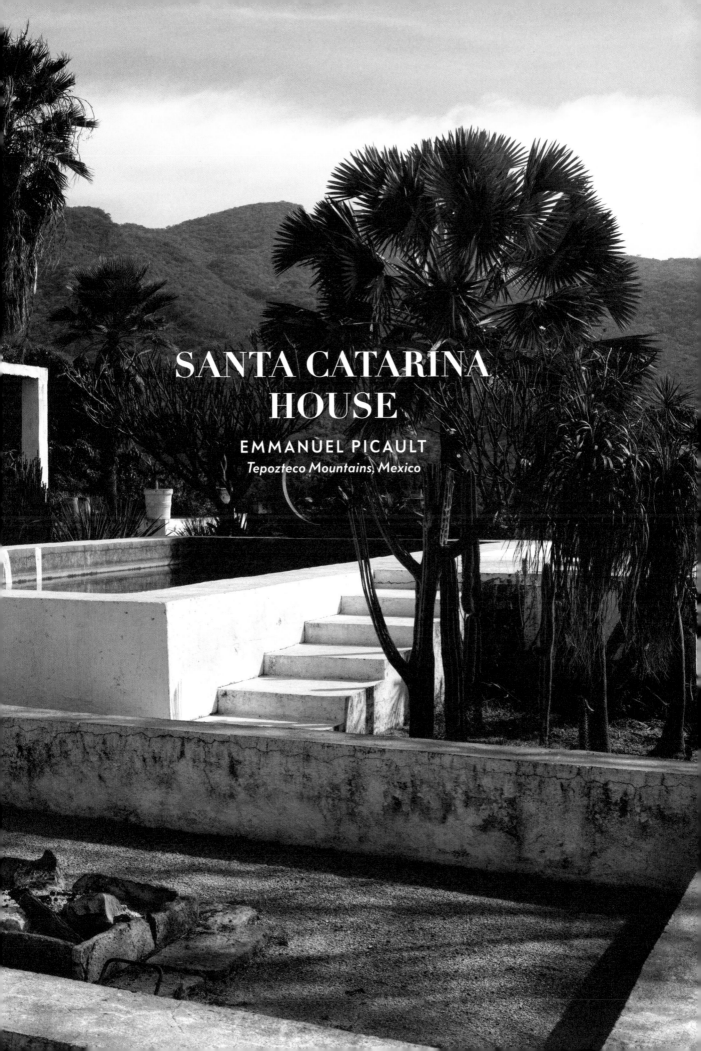

SANTA CATARINA HOUSE

EMMANUEL PICAULT
Tepozteco Mountains, Mexico

WHILE GROWING UP IN A NINTH-century Viking town in Normandy, designer Emmanuel Picault would tell his parents that what he wanted to be when he grew up was Mexican. He'd been interested in archaeology from a young age and was particularly fascinated by the cities of the Maya and the Aztec, great civilizations half a world away from home. In the late 1980s, at the age of seventeen, Picault traveled to Mexico for the first time, spending months as a backpacker in the Maya zones of the Yucatán Peninsula and Chiapas, with forays across the border into Guatemala and Belize. "That trip was absolutely fundamental in the formation of my eye, my feelings, everything," he says. By twenty-six, Picault decided to move to Mexico "y hacerme mexicano, chingado"—regional slang for "and make myself Mexican, damn it." As the beloved Costa Rica–born Mexican chanteuse Chavela Vargas once said, "Mexicans are born wherever the hell we please."

A year after arriving in Mexico City in 2000, Picault founded his design practice and gallery, Chic by Accident, and filled it with antique objects and furnishings encountered in markets across the city. More than a designer, Picault describes himself as an ensemblier, meaning "one who puts together." He adored his new home but quickly realized that "to live in Mexico City, you need to escape often." Around 2006, he found a modest adobe house from the 1930s with a gracious garden in the village of Yautepec, about an hour south of Mexico City, in the neighboring state of Morelos. A few years later, the gardener brought Picault to a family member's quinceañera in the nearby village of Santa Catarina, a small agricultural community at the western extreme of the Tepozteco, a sacred mountain with sheer, forest-draped rock faces crowned with a late-fifteenth-century Aztec temple. "The village has no traffic; it has no exit point," Picault recalls of his first visit. "It was small; it was secret."

OPPOSITE: A daybed in one of the many undefined, unprogrammed spaces that constitute the house, making it equally viable for solitary escapes from the city and for weekend-long revels with friends.

In total, the house can sleep some twenty people scattered among formal bedrooms, like this one, open galleries, and multi-use rooms where Picault rolls out mattresses and blankets for open-air naps.

A space-dividing screen references the formal ingenuity of the glyphs used to record and transmit history in the Maya civilization of Southern Mexico, a subject of fascination for Picault since his childhood.

While strolling the village's periphery, he eventually came upon a forty-foot-high retaining wall lofting a largely inactive piece of farmland and a pair of hangars for tractors. After negotiating a purchase with the owner, Picault tore out the hangars and, before anything, built a pool. "I wanted to be able to design my house while bathing and thinking, thinking, thinking," he says. Those aquatic beginnings were fitting for the fluid, spontaneous design process that still defines the house. The first stage began with Picault buying volcanic stone from nearby quarries—perhaps three metric tons per week—and drawing out plans on the ground using powdered lime. The gardener from Yautepec who'd first brought him to Santa Catarina—he and his son are the only people to have worked on the house's construction—would use these as a guide. "A week later, I would come back and—poof! There would be a wall!" Picault says.

After the walls came rough concrete columns that, three years later, would support the house's flat concrete roof. In the intervening years, Picault painted the walls and columns white and hung black shade cloth, the kind used in the plant nurseries that line the highways around Morelos, to obstruct the mountain sun. He threw up a haphazard roof over one room in the house to use as storage for his few basic furnishings and had them brought out only on weekends, when he would leave the city. "It was a fantastic kind of nomadism," he says. Even after adding the roof, he left the apertures for doors and windows open to the elements and the house's layout flexible and intuitive. The house reads as an archaeological site, a work either in progress or abandoned half-built.

There are no strict bedrooms or rigidly placed furnishings but, rather, adaptable spaces strewn with carpets and mattresses and cushions such that guests—the house can sleep up to twenty people—can go to bed wherever they like, be it on the roof or in the gallery or alongside the pool. "I wake up super early, often at five a.m., and I get to discover my friends before they wake up, which, to me, is the most intimate thing—to see your loved ones at rest."

This flexibility has continued over the years as the house has transformed with and through time. As grass grew over a mound of construction debris, like a half-destroyed pyramid slowly incorporated into the earth, Picault realized that the new topographic feature offered the best view of the house framed by the mountains, so he built an open-sided dining pavilion there from concrete. What was once flat pastureland is now a garden that goes dormant in the dry months of winter and bursts with life come summer. Inside, Picault has allowed one wall, some sixty-five feet long, to grow over with native mosses and lichens that flush with an impossible gradient of greens when the annual rains begin.

"I don't think of this as a house. It's a territory where I can welcome my most intimate friends for moments of celebration, reflection, and sometimes sadness," Picault says. "We read, we listen to music, we tend to the garden, we nap. We cook; there are bonfires; we spend long, long nights in the gallery and the garden." During the Covid-19 pandemic, Picault excavated an eighty-person amphitheater near the retaining wall at the edge of the plot. There, he and his friends now read poetry and perform plays they've written earlier the same day. The whole project, Picault says, stems from "the will to create a space that allows for the greatest possible liberty: liberty of the body and of the spirit, for moments that are beautiful or difficult."

For now, there are still no plans or elevations. Picault hopes to draw them when the house is finished, which it emphatically—and joyously—is not. Archaeological sites never are. They always have new secrets and new intimacies to reveal, stories apt for perpetual retelling.

The first element that the French Mexican designer Emmanuel Picault designed for his country house outside Mexico City was the pool, the place from which he conceptualized the rest of the project's open-ended, flexible structure.

NEXT PAGES: An open pavilion with views to the Tepozteco Mountains.

OPPOSITE: Picault designed the house piecemeal, buying heaps of volcanic stone, like that used for the wall pictured here, from local quarries.

Assembled from local basalt rock, the house resembles, at once, an Aztec ruin, a colonial hacienda with its outer layer of plaster missing, and a modernist house from Mexico's mid-century efflorescence.

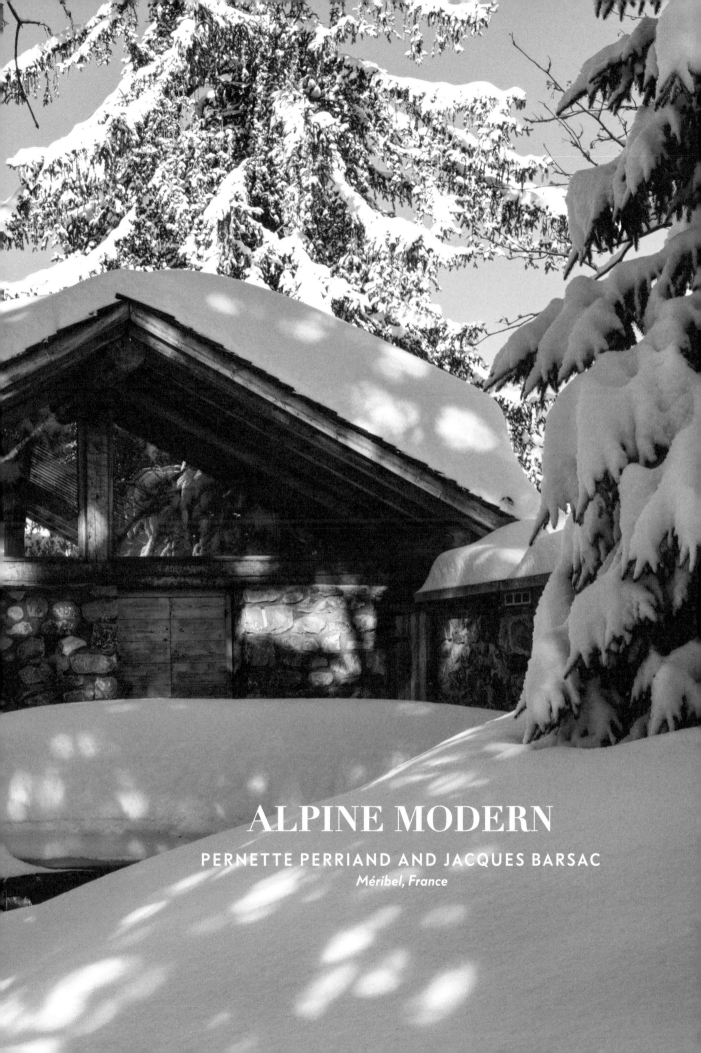

ALPINE MODERN

PERNETTE PERRIAND AND JACQUES BARSAC
Méribel, France

IN JUNE 1936, AFTER WIDESPREAD strikes across France, the newly installed Popular Front government signed the landmark Matignon Accords, guaranteeing workers twelve days of paid annual vacation. It was a transformative moment in the history of labor rights, in the history of France, and in the history of the Alps. That year, six hundred thousand people traveled to visit the country's villages, beaches, and mountains, landscapes that most of the urban working class had never seen before. The Alpine highlands of the Haute-Savoie, with their craggy peaks and stone-walled chalets, would need a new architecture to reflect that transformation: economical, egalitarian, dignified, and modern. Charlotte Perriand, the Parisian architect and designer, was ready.

Perriand had been an enthusiast of Alpine sports since 1925, when she started training as a mountaineer under one of the foremost guides of the period, a man "called the Pope for the depth of his knowledge of the mountains," says Jacques Barsac, Perriand's son-in-law and author of a three-volume catalogue raisonné of her work. Beginning in 1927, Perriand had worked closely with Le Corbusier and his cousin Jean Jeanneret in designing iconic furniture from tubular steel and integrating painting, mural, and textile into epoch-shaping interiors that were at once vigorously forward-looking and deeply tactile, focused equally on pleasure and functionality.

Throughout the 1930s, Perriand designed prefabricated Alpine shelters and daring modernist hotels. "She always linked the mountains with her practice," Barsac says. "All the characteristics of life in the mountains were there in her work: equality of men and women, teamwork and cooperation, challenges and adventure, and the need to persist to the end." Many projects from this period remained on paper or

Examples of Perriand's genius for efficiency: a daybed that doubles as a sleeping area for guests and a movable wooden box that serves as a first tread in the staircase connecting the house's two levels.

The cleverly designed kitchenette harks back to Perriand's early designs for pre-fabricated mountain shelters, conceived for alpinists in need of overnight retreats on extended hikes.

were built only as prototypes. Their bold aesthetic, free from regionalist ornament, was too advanced for bourgeois taste. Perriand was a visionary, far ahead of her time.

In 1940, shortly after the German occupation of Paris, Perriand left France to work in Japan, returning home six years later after a detour through Vietnam, where she waited out the war. Before long, she was back in her beloved Savoie to work on an ill-starred resort in the village of Méribel. When the British developer ran out of money, he offered to pay Perriand with land. She chose a plot in a meadow sheltered by firs and aspens and bounded by a mountain stream. More than a decade later, in 1961, she finally built her refuge in the woods, a delicate compromise between tradition and modernity, between community and isolation— a pure expression of her singular aesthetic.

Though Perriand's initial design involved an inclined roof covered in vegetation—a gesture adapted from her first hotels, themselves inspired by traditional Norwegian houses—local ordinances required gabled roofs, the typological precedents of the Savoie. "After the project was rejected, she went for walks in the villages of the region," says Pernette Perriand, Charlotte's daughter and Barsac's wife. "She took the architecture of those houses and barns and farmsteads and combined that with bare stone walls where you could see the structure."

Instead of an outward show of modernity, Perriand transformed the chalet, with its two modest floors of just 430 square feet each, in subtler ways. By using double-paned glass, a new technology that insulated against the cold, she opened huge apertures in the heavy stone walls to bring the landscape inside, practically erasing the boundaries between wilderness and home. On the lower floor, she embedded the house's primary social space in the hillside with an open hearth at its center.

Upstairs, glass panels under the gables created a sense of breadth even while wood paneling and stone drew the space in close. Sliding wood panels could reorganize the room in seconds, hiding a nook where guests sometimes slept or the metal countertops of an efficient kitchenette. Woven straw floor mats evoked the elegant logic of Japanese design while gesturing to the hay lofts that occupy the upper levels of traditional Savoyard houses. Perriand installed her bedroom under windows carefully placed to draw in the first warming beams of morning light.

For Perriand, the chalet was "a place where she could reload her energies and reconnect with her creativity," Barsac says. But she never conceived of it as an ascetic retreat. The house was always filled with music and cooking and card games, with family and friends—the carpenters and craftsmen who'd helped build the house and the farmers who were their neighbors. At the first of her mother's parties, Pernette recalls, when Charlotte lit the fire, the flue wouldn't draw, and the house filled with smoke. "It was unbearable to be in there, so everyone had to go outside, and it was terribly cold," she says now. "It was really funny to just see smoke pouring out of the house on the first day. You can imagine everyone outside, their eyes all teary." She laughs at the memory, at the decades of memories the house contains. "Everyone remembers the opening party of Charlotte's chalet."

Since 2016, the chalet has been formally protected as a historic monument, preserved from the time of its construction but in no way a relic. It remains as alive as it has ever been, a piece of history still full of song and light.

On the house's wood-paneled upper level, tatami mat floors gesture toward Perriand's time working in Japan just before the country entered World War II as well as to the hay lofts that traditionally occupied the upper eaves of Savoyard houses.

OPPOSITE: Thick stone walls gesture toward the local vernacular of Savoyard barn houses.

Vast windows bring the landscape in, a development made possible by the incorporation of double-paned glass, a new technology at the time and a prime of example of Perriand's intuitive understanding of industrial materials.

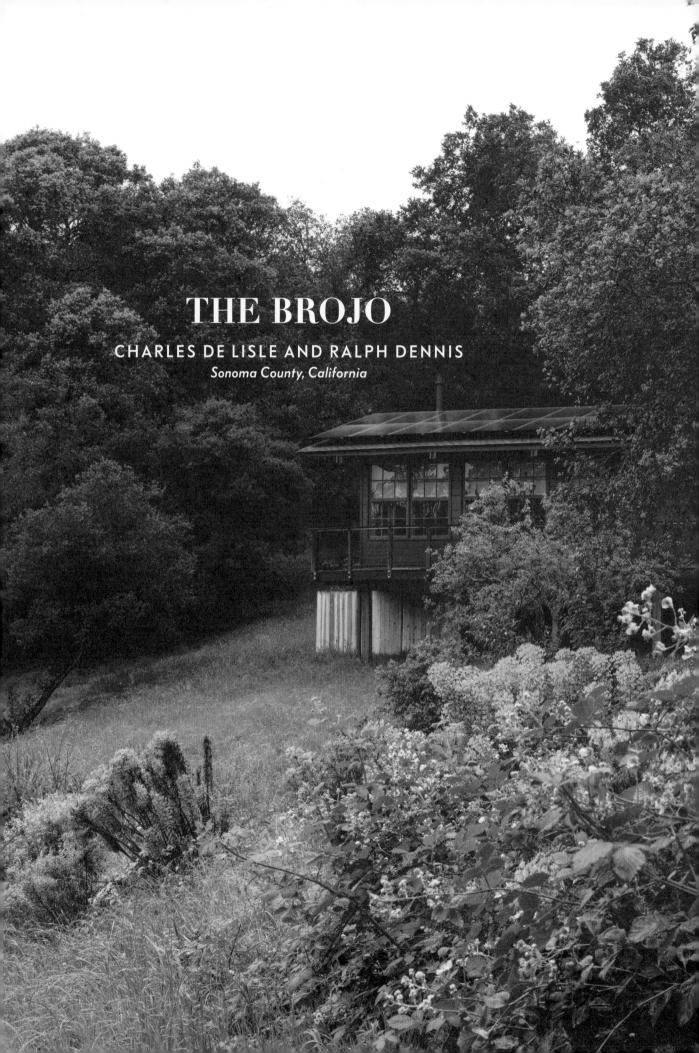

THE BROJO

CHARLES DE LISLE AND RALPH DENNIS
Sonoma County, California

IN THE SUMMER OF 2019, WHEN INTE-rior designer Charles de Lisle was planting the garden around his recently restored cabin in rural Sonoma County, California, he entered the front gate to find the house—originally an outbuilding for a two-bedroom home, which remains in shambles—suddenly crested with a dazzle of bright green leaves. At first, he says, he assumed that new plants had arrived from the nursery. But soon it clicked: a tree had fallen and, propped up by a felicitously placed branch, come to rest gently on the house's eaves. "I thought, 'Well, I guess it's time to call a friend and get out the chainsaw,'" he says now with an unconcerned smirk. Surprises like these, he says, are part and parcel of life in the woods. "There's something nice about the non-permanence of it all," he says, "about *feeling* how uncontrollable nature really is."

De Lisle spent his childhood in the low-slung mountains of Massachusetts, near its border with New Hampshire. Northern Califor-nia, where he has lived for thirty years, bristles with wildness of a different order. Since buying their land in 2018—their second time purchas-ing property in the region—de Lisle and his partner, interior designer Ralph Dennis, have found gargantuan paw prints left by a moun-tain lion stalking the edge of the lot and have hung mesh barriers in the corners of the cabin, in a "constant battle to keep out all the living things that want to come inside," de Lisle says.

It was this forced contact with the outdoors that had always attracted de Lisle to Sonoma. He'd toyed with the idea of buying land here since the late 1990s, but it wasn't until 2012 that he and Dennis bought their first Sonoma cabin, an off-grid kit house near Sebastopol, one val-ley inland from the Pacific. He and Dennis had, through the years, worked together on a couple of houses for themselves, but the Sonoma house was to be entirely de Lisle's project. "I make a

The house's main room, lined with ply, acts as a
bedroom, living space, and kitchen.

living making other people's houses beautiful,"
de Lisle says. "I wanted to do something without
anyone else's criteria," he says.

De Lisle grew up in a house his father built
by hand and spent much of his childhood in the
woods building forts and teepees, "so, building
a house was something I always wanted to do."
The Sebastopol property, cut off from basic
infrastructure, proved too challenging a spot
to realize that dream. Then, one afternoon in
2016, driving west toward Napa, de Lisle and
Dennis got lost on a single-lane road lined by
pastureland and vineyards. It reminded him
of the narrow country lane where he'd been
raised. "It just felt viscerally right," he says. Two
years later, they sold the land and Sebastopol house to buy a ten-acre lot off that road,
complete with a modest house, a nineteenth-
century barn, and a handful of outbuildings in
varying states of decay.

The previous tenants, renters who farmed
marijuana, had left the site littered with plastic
hoses, concrete blocks, and a mountain of dis-
posable planters. The owner before them had
left rusted-out bird cages from a peacock farm
and the remains of an exuberant water garden,
which de Lisle and Dennis exhumed from a for-
bidding hedge of wild blackberry. De Lisle and
Dennis uncovered, too, the flimsy cabin—gen-
erously sized at 950 square feet, but thrown
together haphazardly—that they decided to
adapt for shelter while de Lisle made the land
habitable.

The cabin, de Lisle says, "was a nightmare,"
its exterior and interior painted black, its plywood
floors red with a twelve-foot-wide yin/yang sym-
bol emblazoned across the center. Whoever had
previously occupied the space had stuffed dirty
laundry into the corners for insulation, installed
a DJ booth, and left the metal hull of a bathtub
out on the porch to oxidize. De Lisle and Dennis hired a contractor who brought on a master

barn builder from Vermont and a shipwright from
New Hampshire.

Together, they insulated the building,
reframed the windows with recycled redwood,
and lined the walls and floors with high-grade
ply, its loose grain like the whorls in marbled
paper. From a dank, dirty hovel, they conjured
a gracious, light-filled home that de Lisle filled
with Berber carpets from Morocco, prototypes
from his own practice, chairs and chaises by the
likes of Hans Wegner and Max Lamb, and a
particularly beloved Joe Colombo clip lamp—
a ragtag yard sale, de Lisle jokes, "of broken
things from designers we love that ended up in
our world."

While his work for other clients tends toward
practicality, the Sonoma cabin has given de
Lisle the space to explore a more spontaneous
and evocative approach. "I like having useless
things, I like to have space for space's sake, I like
how stuff feels," he says. For the cabin's doors, he
insisted on rustic screens with creaking springs
whose wooden frames slap shut like bear traps.
When he and Dennis installed a pool two years
back, de Lisle made the patio from stones set
into over-washed cement, meant to evoke the
mineral smell of his childhood swimming hole in
Massachusetts and the harsh texture of concrete
infill at rocky beaches on the Italian Riviera. "It's
the most uncomfortable, tactile thing," he says
with relish.

For now, de Lisle has abandoned his dream
of building a house from scratch, preferring
instead the labor of restoring his land. "It's a
do-something-on-the-land-or-do-nothing kind
of place," he jokes. When he takes on the main
house, now used for storage, he'll strip away
what's rotten and restore what he can. "It's a bit
of my Yankee heritage," he says, flinty and wry.
"If something's broken, you fix it."

OPPOSITE: A massive picture window beside the bathtub opens onto the surrounding forest.

A vintage stacking chair by Robert Mallet-Stevens stands beside a door of reclaimed redwood in the bath house.

Built into a cement deck, the pool was meant to evoke the sense memory of the smell of wet concrete during the humid East Coast summers of de Lisle's childhood.

Fog settles in over a meadow in Sonoma.

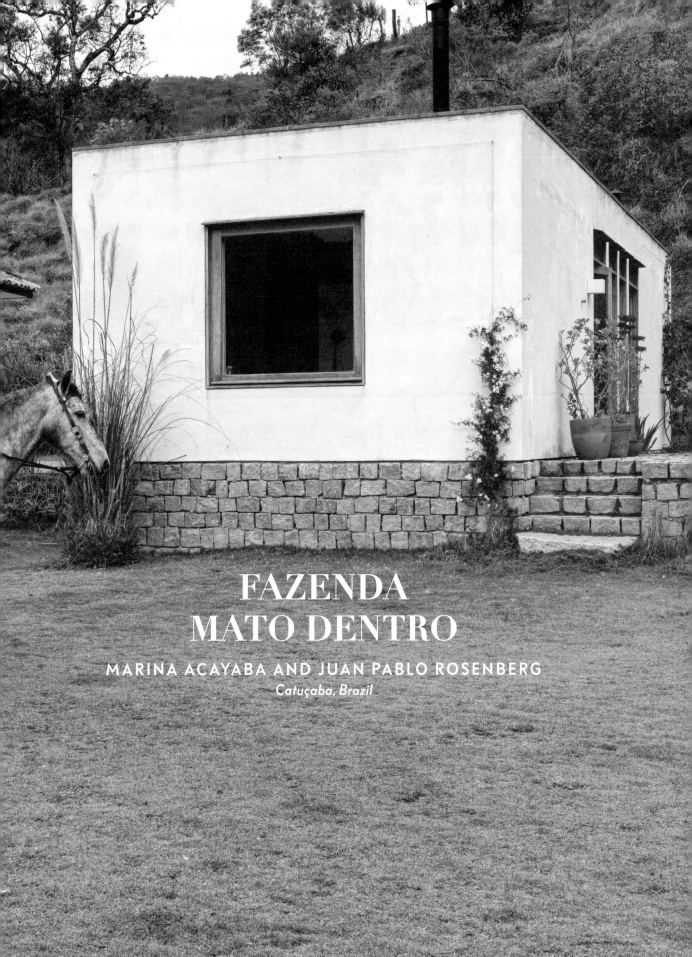

FAZENDA
MATO DENTRO

MARINA ACAYABA AND JUAN PABLO ROSENBERG
Catuçaba, Brazil

FOR CENTURIES, THE LAND ROUTE between Rio de Janeiro and São Paulo, today Brazil's two largest cities, has run through an inland valley shielded from the sea by high mountains densely cloaked in tropical forest. Off that road, narrow dirt tracks, transitable only on horseback, wound between small villages, subsistence farms, and, outside the village of Catuçaba, the pilgrimage site of the Basilica de Nossa Senhora Aparecida. It was near here that the father of Maria Martins (no relation to the modernist sculptor of the same name) built a modest, 915-square-foot farmhouse in 1890, the same house where Martins fed pilgrims and raised twenty children (some of them biologically hers, most of them adopted) and the same house that, in 2018, the São Paulo–based architects Marina Acayaba and Juan Pablo Rosenberg would buy and transform into a second home.

By then, Catuçaba and the surrounding valleys had become absolute backwaters, dominated by grazing cattle and small farmsteads. In the second half of the twentieth century, as São Paulo's population continued to explode—it is now the continent's largest city by far—authorities built a major highway connecting the country's vibrant mercantile capital with the glamorous seaside metropolis of Rio de Janeiro, the nation's capital until 1960. "This place was stopped in time," says Rosenberg, whose family fled the brutal dictatorship in his native Argentina when he was an infant. "It was no longer on the way to anywhere for anybody."

Acayaba and Rosenberg came across the house in 2015, though they'd visited Catuçaba for the first time two years earlier. "Since I was a kid, I've always loved farms and mountains. I never liked the beach," says Acayaba, who grew up in São Paulo in a family of architects. (Her father, Marcos, is a living luminary of the city's architectural scene; her mother, Marlene, wrote the first seminal study on Paulista houses.) "I was always searching for a place like

A local restorer who'd worked on rebuilding heritage structures in a nearby village following a devastating flood designed custom casings to fit window frames distorted by time like this one in the house's living room.

A rocking chair by São Paulo–based designer Carlos Motta strikes a dynamic contrast with the rough lime-washed surfaces of restored wattle-and-daub walls.

The twin guest suites in the house's annex echo the material simplicity of the original farmhouse but in a contemporary dialect, with smooth white plaster and earthenware floor tiles of local manufacture.

this." On their 2013 visit to Catuçaba—at the time, it was virtually untouched by outsiders—Acayaba and Rosenberg fell in love with the region, which is, for most of the year, hot and dry. In 2015, friends in the area alerted them to the old Martins house, abandoned for the previous few years and inhabited for ten years before that by a family in the employ of the owner, a local sheriff. It took nearly three years to negotiate the sale of the house.

Almost immediately after taking ownership in 2018, Acayaba and Rosenberg started restoring the house. "When we came here, we had a really strong feeling that we shouldn't change anything, because it would destroy the soul of the place," Acayaba says. "The idea of this woman, Maria Martins . . . Her presence was so strong that we felt we really had to ask permission to inhabit the place." Set on nearly three hundred acres, the house is almost entirely isolated. At night, Acayaba and Rosenberg say, you can't see a single light. The nearest neighbors are all descendants of Maria Martins, constant reminders of her powerful presence and influence. Uphill from the house, a cross marks the place where Martins and her family built a small chapel to commemorate the miraculous apparition of a crucifix on her kitchen ceiling, a white mark untouched by the soot that rose from a wood-burning stove. (Electricity arrived in the valley around 2005.) A mischievous character from Brazilian folklore known as Saci wanders the valley playing tricks on people and killing off livestock for sport. "People around here believe really strongly in these stories."

To restore the house, Rosenberg and Acayaba hired craftspeople who had rebuilt the nearby heritage town of São Luíz do Paraitinga after a devastating flood in 2010. Using the original constructive technique, called *pau a pique* (in English, "wattle and daub"), they repaired the house's uneven walls

by caking earth over a wooden lattice frame and whitewashing it with lime. In old pictures the owners found onsite, they discovered a six-foot-high stone wall that had once enclosed a platform on which the house was built; unearthing the upper edge of the wall, they reshaped the landscape into subtle terraces, one for the domestic space, another just below now dominated by a broad brick patio with a fire pit at its center. Built from perishable materials, the house had leaned and tilted over the years, distorting the windows and door frames. In order to respect these imperfections, Rosenberg and Acayaba had windows custom-fitted to their crooked casements.

Yet, for all their rigor and care in restoring the original structure, Acayaba says, "when we first got here, it wasn't very cozy. Or, no, not cozy. It wasn't a *place*. It was just a house in the middle of the valley. So, we decided to create an environment for the house." To do that, the couple designed a second structure, a simple rectangular volume parallel to the original house and connected to it by an open patio paved with handmade earthenware tiles traditional to the region. Bisecting the patio, a narrow channel of water recalls Mughal gardens and Louis Kahn's Salk Institute reduced to a domestic scale. The new structure, which houses a pair of guest suites, is "very prismatic and minimalist," Rosenberg says. It also repeats many of the materials of the original structure: the lime-slaked walls, the pediment of stone recovered from a nearby house in demolition. The open terrace formed between the two volumes has become a kind of open-air living room, a common space that connects the buildings to each other and to the expansive landscape that surrounds them.

While Acayaba and Rosenberg subtly reshaped the environment around the house—called Fazenda Mato Dentro, or Inner Forest Farm—the countryside has also begun to

reshape their life in the city. Growing greens, onions, radishes, and herbs in a pair of kitchen gardens and raising dairy cows, chickens, and pigs has allowed Acayaba and Rosenberg and their three young children to start distancing themselves from Brazil's agricultural industry. The family buys cheese from Maria Martins's grandson and might trade cuts of a recently slaughtered pig for help with repairing the roof or caring for their horses while they're in the city.

The spiritual distance between the city and country has begun to shrink in subtler ways as well. "Last year we discovered a beautiful story of our own," says Acayaba. "We were looking into my great-grandfather's journals, and we found out that his first farm here in Brazil was called Mato Dentro, the same as ours. When his wife died, he renamed it for her, so no one in our family ever knew the original name, but that really amazed us." She shook her head, still wondering at the coincidence, as Rosenberg shrugged and smiled, a rationalist happily acquiescing to enchantment. "We're starting our own legends."

The village of Catuçaba and its surroundings lie deep in the mountains that separate Brazil's inland savannahs from its long Atlantic Coast. Much native forest has been lost to cattle ranching through the years, a trend Acayaba and Rosenberg hope to reverse.

Horses follow a path through young forest growing
back after years languishing as pastureland.

DIE ES HOUSE

GABRIEL AND GWEN FAGAN
Cape Town, South Africa

PREVIOUS PAGES: The sweeping roof of the Die Es House suggests the waves on the South Atlantic while its towering chimney gestures toward the archetypal forms of Cape Dutch farmhouses built in the countryside around Cape Town, South Africa.

The hearth that lends the house its name—*die es* in Afrikaans—was big enough for the entire family to gather within it.

IN 1964, THE ARCHITECT GABRIEL Fagan and his wife, Gwen, bought a plot of land high on a hillside in the seaside suburb of Camps Bay. Set on a scrubby slope between the frigid Atlantic coast and the soaring cliff faces known as the Twelve Apostles, Camps Bay was, at the time, mostly a weekend destination for residents of the city center, which is located northwest over the saddle that separates the conical spire of Lion's Head from the flat-topped promontory of Table Mountain. Despite its spectacular views, Camps Bay was considered barely habitable due to the gusts of gale-force winds that barrel down the mountainside on their way to the sea. But the Fagans, who'd recently moved with their four young children from a rural farmstead outside the distant inland capital of Pretoria, did not shy away from challenges.

Both Gwen, rapidly approaching one hundred, and Gabriel, better known as "Gawie"— who died in 2020 at the age of ninety-four—had come from unconventional families. Gawie's father, as chief justice of South Africa, gave his name to the 1946 Fagan Commission, which argued (in the end, unsuccessfully) against the imposition of South Africa's most brutal apartheid laws; many of his other relatives were famed musicians and actors. Gwen, meanwhile, was raised from ages two to eight by an uncle on the family farm before going to live with her single mother, a voice teacher in the university town of Stellenbosch, and, Gwen claims, "the first Bohemian woman in South Africa." In town, Gwen planted a vegetable garden behind the second-floor flat she shared with her mother, attacking the dry soil with pails of water and a stick. When her mother was diagnosed with cancer, Gwen chose to study medicine, unusual for a woman in the 1940s; she met Gawie while at university. Distrustful of men due to her own absent father, Gwen made Gawie wait years before their first kiss.

Upon their arrival in Camps Bay, the young couple rented an apartment down the hill from

The exquisite joinery in the kitchen's custom cabinetry
is matched by the rich, cobalt blue of the backsplash,
also custom-made in Gawie's favorite hue.

their land and sold their Fiat to buy a second-hand concrete mixer. For two and a half years, they walked up and down the slope almost daily as they built their home from scratch. Each of the children was given a job "according to size and ability," says Gwen: "The littlest one had the hose, the next one up handled the sand, and the bigger ones went back and forth with the wheelbarrow." As a family, they laid brick, put up rebar, and poured cement, basing the entirety of the house's design on a sketch Gawie had scratched out, in a fit of inspiration, on a flight between Cape Town and Pretoria. They moved in, at the children's insistence, before they'd completed the upper floor or installed the picture windows that seal the living room off from the landscape. At night, they would tie their blankets to makeshift bed frames to keep them from blowing off.

In its basic contours, the house captured the simplicity and economy of means the Fagans so admired in their country's rural vernacular. They had seen it in the squat earthen houses of the Karoo Desert and in the Cape Dutch farmhouses scattered around Cape Town's hinterlands, with their lime-washed walls and sculptural chimney stacks rising like sentinels. On the second floor, a straight hallway connected the four modest bedrooms and two bathrooms, while, downstairs, on the house's entry level, the open-plan living, dining, and kitchen space centered on the vast fireplace that lends the house its name: "Die Es," Afrikaans for "the Hearth."

Above all, Gwen says, "Gawie's work was based on the natural environment." Die Es was no exception; prototypically modern in its transparency, it was also deeply imbued with the spirit and materials of the Western Cape. One day, while walking in the mountains not far from the construction site for a new road being etched into the cliffs, Gwen and Gawie came across a giant boulder of yellow sandstone;

that boulder, broken down into tiles, became the entry stair that connects the carport at street level to the main doorway several feet below. The stones set into the gentle slope of the entry hall, hand-laid by Gwen, came out of the ground when they excavated the house's foundations. She also tore out the exotic plants that had established themselves on the lot and, with the help of her oldest child, Henry, replaced them with a garden of native shrubs that now embrace the house in a dense tapestry of verdigris and emerald. Even the house's sinuous roofline, its most poetic and formally daring gesture, was inspired by the waves that roll into shore far below; it seems also to echo, if distantly, the silhouette of the mountains that rear up behind it.

Even more than the sea or the mountains, the house reflects the brilliant, eccentric lives lived within it. Gawie, who participated five times in the annual sailing race from Cape Town to Rio, brought his love of the sea to the rounded corners of the bathroom doors and to the pendant lights made from antique Japanese fishing buoys, their pale blue surfaces an echo of the brise-soleil panels that protect the windows on the house's rear. The elevated platform that connects the living room to an outdoor patio—crowded with Gwen's prized collection of succulents and pelargoniums—used to double as a stage where the family would put on recitals for friends. A towering black stain behind the hearth marks almost sixty years of family gatherings, while the bookshelves at the far end of the room are crowded with titles written by family and friends, their spines faded by decades of blazing crimson sunsets.

When Gawie died, he and Gwen had been together for seventy-two years, fifty-five of them spent in the Die Es house. In 1969, Gwen left her medical practice to join Gawie's office as a landscape designer and as the principal archival

A sewing table in the second-floor hallway, specially designed by Gawie for Gwen.

One of the house's four spartan bedrooms, its east-facing window looking onto the steep promontories of the Twelve Apostles.

researcher for the more than two hundred restoration projects they would complete during his lifetime. Gwen, with no formal training in the field, became one of the foremost experts on South African roses long before earning a PhD in landscape architecture in 1995, "just to make sure that I knew what I was talking about," she says now. In the late 1980s, when she and Gawie created a massive compendium of the flowers she'd spent years studying, publishers refused to print the book because of its size and cost, a result of Gawie's exquisite photos, as delicate as eighteenth-century botanical drawings, and Gwen's insistence that the images be printed at one-to-one scale. The Fagans' response was to found their own publishing house and print the book themselves.

Set on the shelf next to Gwen and Gawie's bed, there's a single rose in a small vase. Years ago, Gwen received a call from South Africa's foremost rosarian asking what she might look for in a flower that would bear her name. "I said, 'Well, it must be big and pink and full, but the most important thing is that it must have a lovely fragrance,'" she recalls now. Sometime later, after a talk at a conference, a woman she'd never met approached her with a pot. In it was a rose plant, its blossoms the pale pink of clouds struck by the first rays of sunset, the same rose on Gwen's bookshelf—the rose that bears her name. She shrugs and smiles at that memory, one of so many held between the walls she and her family built. "I'm just lucky," she says.

OPPOSITE: The living room's bookshelves are lined with titles by friends and acquaintances.

A simple gate connects the house's entry to the garden of native plants that Gwen, with help from her eldest son Henry, planted here during the house's construction.

OPPOSITE: The bedspread in Gawie and Gwen's bedroom is a keepsake from Mexico; the rose on the windowsill is an example of the cultivar that bears Gwen's name.

CASA LOS NOPALES

JOSE DÁVILA
San Gabriel, Mexico

PREVIOUS PAGES: The house consists of three separate volumes, with the central structure, pictured here, turned to face the precise center point between the Nevado de Colima and the Volcán de Colima.

Dávila's house faces south toward a pair of volcanic peaks, one active, one dormant.

EARLY ONE MORNING IN THE AUTUMN of 2013, artist Jose Dávila went out for a walk in the scrubby hill country outside the village of San Gabriel in the rugged sierra. Dávila, among the country's most consequential contemporary sculptors, had started searching for land here five years before, driving up on weekends from his home in Guadalajara, Jalisco's capital, and until recently Mexico's second-largest city, to stay with friends who would take him out to scour the surrounding countryside. On that particular morning, a Sunday, he'd arrived early and decided to set off on his own while he waited for his host to wake up. Not far from the house, he stumbled upon a view he'd never seen so clearly in this part of Jalisco: a pair of volcanoes, the extinct and ice-capped Nevado de Colima and the active Volcán de Colima, in perfect relief on the horizon. As Dávila stood there, a puff of ash rose from the Volcán de Colima, or the Volcán de Fuego—Volcano of Fire—as it's sometimes called. "It was a bolt

of clarity, almost an epiphany," he says now. "I thought right then, 'This has to be the spot.'"

Born and raised in Guadalajara, Dávila felt profoundly connected to the austere landscape in this particular corner of Jalisco's hills. Whereas the nearby town of Tapalpa, a popular holiday destination for families from the city, was well known for its pine forests and rustic charm, the land here was arid, the flora stunted by rocky soil. As an adolescent, he'd come here to camp with friends. He'd also been raised with a clear vision of this as the emblematic landscape of the Mexican countryside, a vision propagated around the world through the films and music of Vicente Fernandez (the classic *macho mexicano* singing romantic lyrics under a blazing sun) and the books of the renowned fiction writer Juan Rulfo, which are set largely in landscapes just like this one, shaped by volcanoes and scrub-land, by harsh shadows and circling buzzards. "It was the wild landscape of Jalisco, agave and nopales"—the prickly pear

cactus from which the house takes its name. "It was Rulfo country," Dávila says, "halfway between ice and fire."

Having studied architecture at Guadalajara's Western Institute of Technology and Higher Studies in the mid-1990s, Dávila briefly considered designing the house himself. He had never practiced architecture, but he had put his training to good use throughout his two-decade career as a sculptor, using gravity as a raw material in monumental works that held slabs of marble and stone, steel beams and planks of wood, in delicate, sometimes precarious-seeming balance, using little more than ratchet straps and the weight of the objects themselves. Still, he says, "it's one thing to have *studied* architecture and something else entirely to *be* an architect."

Out of "respect for the discipline," he says, he chose to collaborate, deciding eventually to work with Juan Palomar, who, as practitioner and teacher, has long served as a bridge between Dávila's generation and that of Luis Barragán, another legendary *Jalisciense*. Like Barragán's, Palomar's work tends to be reticent and clean, with a close connection to techniques and materials of the countryside—the ranchero sensibility of frankness and clarity that Dávila was seeking. "In all of my work, the balance and use of gravity is completely real, so transparency and honesty are really important to my use of materials," Dávila says. "That's part of what I find so original in ranchero buildings: There are no tricks; they use materials as they are."

Aside from using GPS to situate the house so that its primary window would face the precise midpoint between the volcanoes, Dávila and Palomar used analog methods throughout the design and construction process. From the first, Dávila insisted that all the plans be drawn by hand. "I didn't use AutoCAD as a student," he says, referring to the software used to create precise two- and three-dimensional drawings.

"Filling in the blue of the sky on an elevation—that meant a half hour of reflection." Palomar loved the idea, though he warned Dávila that to complete the house without computer-generated plans would mean weekly visits to resolve problems and questions onsite. Later, Dávila's friend Paco Gutiérrez, founder of the Guadalajara-based CoA Arquitectura, made formal plans to manage the fine-tuned details of the kitchen, bathrooms, and herringbone floors made from a dark Mexican hardwood called *tzalam*. (Dávila refused to look at them until after construction was complete.)

To lay the house's foundations, Dávila and Palomar excavated into the site's pale purple flagstone, pieces of which the artist eventually incorporated into a public artwork for one of Guadalajara's parks. The main house—two other volumes contain the primary suite and a pair of guest rooms, respectively—sits low on the site, its eighteen-inch-thick brick walls covered with a rough, gray plaster of lime, local soil, and river sand. A gabled roof covered in terracotta tiles rests on exposed beams, a gesture of humility toward the regional vernacular. A terrace of flagstone from the nearby village of Juanacatlán, its cobbles laid painstakingly with the flat sides facing up, opens out around the structures—inspired as much by the puzzle-like land art of British sculptor Richard Long as by a simple taquería where Dávila used to stop on the road from Guadalajara into the mountains. (It's since been replaced by a convenience store.)

Within the house, Dávila eschewed the usual self-conscious markers of rusticity—the heavy wood and painted tiles that tip so quickly into pastiche—in favor of creating "a space that would erase the configuration of an urban house, where you would feel, after driving two hours from home, like you'd arrived someplace different." While Dávila afforded himself plenty of luxuries—a Wolf stove in the kitchen, where he often spends hours cooking, and a wine cellar set into the rough stone walls and gravel floors of the basement—he also opened the house to the elements. To go from the living room to his own bedroom, for instance, Dávila has to cross the patio, no matter if it's raining or cold. "I wanted to see the stars at night," he says. "Comfort and functionality were never going to dictate the solutions here."

Though Dávila plans to build a studio on the site eventually, for the time being, the house serves as a place of reflection and—this being Jalisco, where the most common way to say "hang out" is with the verb *cotorrear,* for "to gab"—a place for gathering friends and family. As with his early training in architecture, the house has clearly nourished Dávila's work, but so has the work nourished the house. There's the block of stone by the hearth, which, during construction, Dávila used as a chair for meetings with contractors and which he now uses as a perch from which to stoke the fire—a sculpture of sorts made useful, as all things must be in a true ranchero house. His sensibility is visible in the careful balance between the house's three structures, each with its own gravitational force, generating tension around open space. It's visible, too, in the jigsaw terrace and, most literally, in the sculpture, made by Dávila and placed at the terrace's far end, near the spot where he first decided to build his home in this precise place.

The sculpture, like the house, is simple, a piece of stone—the color of rust, the shape of an anvil—balanced at the edge of a concrete prism that doubles as a bench. Behind it, mountains recede to the south. Volcanoes pierce the horizon. Together with the house and the hills, it stands in dynamic equipoise, frozen between stillness and motion, ice and fire, permanence and ephemerality—a memorial to an epiphany.

OPPOSITE: A chimney drops like a periscope, alongside a chair from Garza Marfa, in the lofted family room in the house's main structure.

The rhythmic silhouette of the main house's staircase echoes those built by the architect Luis Barragán, whose influence is clearly visible in Dávila's house and in contemporary homes throughout Jalisco, where the Pritzker laureate grew up.

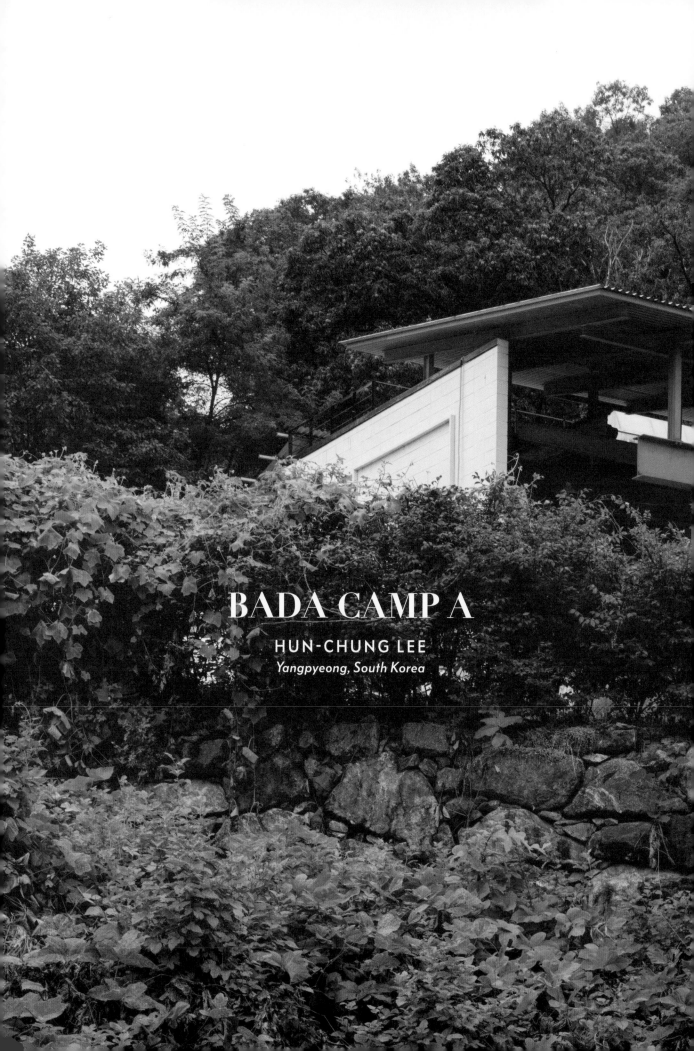

BADA CAMP A

HUN-CHUNG LEE
Yangpyeong, South Korea

PREVIOUS PAGES: Hulking red steel beams, like a temple gate at a Confucian shrine, mark the entrance of the studio space, pictured here, at the ceramicist Hun-chung Lee's home in the mountains east of Seoul, South Korea.

Exposed wood beams and wooden floors lend warmth to the house's dining room and kitchen, otherwise sheathed in hard, cool concrete.

"I'M NOT A VERY ORGANIZED PERSON," says South Korean ceramicist Hun-chung Lee. "When I have a strong feeling about something, I make decisions very quickly." This was how he chose, as a young man, to study art and how he chose, while in his second year of art school, to take on ceramics as his major. His swift instincts drove him to move from Seoul to San Francisco in 1993 to pursue a graduate degree in sculpture. When he returned home three years later, in 2002, he followed those instincts to a piece of land in the mountains east of Seoul, where he would build his home and studio, a space, he hoped, where he might work in solitude.

Lee had gone to Yangpyeong, a popular retreat about thirty miles from the sprawling South Korean capital, to visit a close friend who had property there, driving two hours from what was then his studio on a relative's deer ranch in a remote area near the demilitarized zone on the border with North Korea. After Lee mentioned his dream of one day building a studio of his own, the friend took him to see a modest parcel of land on a wooded slope that the friend—the plot's owner, as it happened—was in no great rush to sell. "I was young, I didn't have the money, and I didn't have enough credit to ask for a loan, so that was the end of the conversation," Lee recalls. "But that night, I couldn't sleep, I couldn't stop thinking about the land." The next day, he and his friend struck a deal: Lee would pay for the land in installments over the course of a year, an atypical arrangement in South Korea, Lee says.

Though he initially planned to build his home with an architect friend who'd offered to design it pro bono, that architect, upon seeing the lot, recommended that Lee offload it as soon as he could. The property was steep—not uncommon in a country where mountains occupy more than two thirds of the land, but still less than ideal from the standpoint of construction. It also faced away from the sun, which would only make the harsh, snowy winters more

The ceramicist's house, pictured here, faces his studio across an open courtyard excavated from the slope of the lot.

difficult to bear. Lee was defiant. "I decided to design it myself. I thought, 'It can't be *that* different from making a sculpture.'"

This rejection of boundaries between media and disciplines has defined Lee's work for years, particularly in his ceramic furniture, whose balloon-like forms in shades of celadon and opal are as ambiguous as the artist is decisive, gleefully ridiculing the generic separation of craft, art, and industrial design. As a student, Lee had only narrowly chosen art over architecture as a means to express his lifelong fascination with a variety of materials. By his second year in school, that fascination had brought him to ceramics. Still, the curriculum at the time was designed "to make technicians," he says. "The burden of all that tradition was too much for me." By then, Lee had for years been interested in the Bay Area's Funk art movement, which, beginning in the late 1950s, had reacted against the inhumanity of abstract expressionism. "I decided to go somewhere I could be free," he says.

After moving back home, he started mounting solo shows at least once each year. In one conceptual show from the early 2000s, he replicated the environment of a living room with sculptures made from various materials, including a C-shaped concrete table with a steel ball hanging from its undercarriage. "When people saw that piece in the context of a gallery, they wanted to know what it *meant*," Lee marvels. But fixed meaning and the preening pretensions of the art world never interested him. "A few years later, I showed the same piece in a design show, and people didn't ask about meaning; they just tried to enjoy it," he says. "That's how I started making furniture, to get closer to my audience."

Those were, and not by coincidence, the same years in which Lee was building his Yangpyeong studio. After dismissing his architect friend from the project, he started to mock up plans, acquiring a topographical map of the lot and molding his ideas from clay. He carved terraces into the hillside and set the home and studio perpendicular to each other, using the two structures as retaining walls to stabilize the excavated land. The studio would open onto the newly flat courtyard through a frame of hulking steel beams, painted red like a *hongsalmun* (a gateway to a Confucian shrine) exploded to an industrial scale. The house, meanwhile, would be both porous and hermetic, its spare interior embraced by walls of perforated concrete and a ceiling of exposed wooden beams. The two volumes would resemble a boulder and a threshold, a rock the mountain had expelled and the void it left behind.

In those years, Lee couldn't afford to hire a full-time contractor. Instead, he managed the building site himself, making the four-hour round trip from his studio five days each week to lead construction while continuing to produce ceramics from his distant kiln. As a result, "the plans changed a lot during the process, the same as when I make sculpture," he says. "As I'm working, I study the form and material, and it changes as I go." While building the house, Lee says, "I learned a lot about welding and carpentry and concrete by making mistakes and fixing them." In 2007, three years after completing the house and studio, he extended the property with a storage and gallery space whose roof became an extension of the grassy courtyard between the original buildings. While the house's interior feels warm and intimate, with its extensive use of plywood and pine, the gallery, with its concrete walls, drain-grate skylights, and columns made from industrial steel tubing, feels more like a bunker or the inside of a dam—the infrastructure to support a growing enterprise.

Today, Lee splits his time between Korea and California, where he has a second studio and a home in Santa Monica. Where

Yangpyeong and the mountains offer him a degree of isolation, California brings him closer to the ocean and the intellectual excitement of Los Angeles. Working between studios, Lee says, has generated surprises in his ceramics, too, shaped as they are by environment and context—by LA's gauzy Pacific light, by the chilly precision of Seoul's cool winter sun, and by the abstract emotional shift he experiences moving from one place to the other.

Though the newest building on the Yangpyeong compound, the gallery is the first to appear along the narrow road Lee himself built twenty years ago to connect the house to town. Embossed in tall block letters in the building's concrete façade are the words BADA (Korean for "ocean" and the name of Lee's company) and CAMP A. "Bada" gestures toward distance, both physical and temporal, to cherished memories of going out to sea with his father, who died when Lee was a teenager. The name "Camp A" makes explicit that this mountainous land, with its steaming summers and snowy winters and endless tides of forested hills, is home.

Journeys remain as important to Lee's work as they were in his youth, yet, for him, the experience of going away has to do with seeking not so much inspiration as a peculiar form of introspection. "I travel to take some distance and look back at myself," he says. "But to make a perfect journey, you have to return. If you don't come back, that's not a journey; that's just *leaving*," Lee says. For him, these mountains are not a place of escape or refuge, as mountains across the world have been for eons, whether for city dwellers clambering for fresh air, revolutionaries and rebels escaping suppression, or holy people seeking enlightenment. For Lee, the mountains are the safe and quiet center of his world. They are his base camp, the ballast for a life guided by tides of intuition, a place where journeys end—and where new ones can always begin.

Stairs made from merbau, an Indonesian timber, rise below a series of paintings by Korean artist Kang-yong Kim.

Lee maintains two studios, one in Santa Monica, where he spends half his time, and the other here in Yangpyeong, which he operates with the help of an on-site production team.

The mountains in the district of Yangpyeong, just east from the sprawling South Korean capital and seen here from the living room, are a popular rural retreat for city dwellers.

NIEMEYER REVISITED

ADRIANA VAREJÃO AND PEDRO BUARQUE
Rio de Janeiro, Brazil

PREVIOUS PAGES: A sculpture by Mexican artist Pedro Reyes stands alongside the house's entrance, a seam of white amid the tropical greenery and the angular summit of Corcovado Hill surmounted by Christ Redeemer in the distance.

Set into the steep granite cliffs that rise behind the house, the lookout, original to Niemeyer's design, offers spectacular views of the Atlantic horizon over the rooftops of Lagoa and Ipanema.

FROM THE TIME OF ITS FOUNDING IN the sixteenth century, Rio de Janeiro has been shaped, confined, and made magnificent by its mountains. In his 1850 memoir, *White-Jacket*, published twenty-eight years after Brazil won its independence, Herman Melville waxed lyrical about Rio's "high conical peaks, which at sunrise and sunset burn like vast tapers" and from which "untiring summer hangs perpetually in terraces of vivid verdure." As Rio grew, its urban footprint seeped into the narrow flatlands between granite bluffs and, later, expanded on landfill excavated from the city's lower hills. Even the iconic beaches of Copacabana and Flamengo were built on mountain soil. Later, settlements known colloquially as favelas ascended the slopes in cubist arrangements of brick, concrete, and tin. Rather than radiating out from a central point, Rio spread around the forest-draped peaks of Tijuca National Park, a mountainous expanse of more than fifteen square miles dotted with orchids and waterfalls and traversed by mountain streams. Rio is, at its literal core, a mountain city. And its most beautiful homes—among them the radiant modernist villa of artist Adriana Varejão and film producer Pedro Buarque—are mountain houses.

Varejão and Buarque first visited what is now their primary residence in 2010, forty-one years after it was designed by the legendary Brazilian modernist Oscar Niemeyer. Built on a modest budget for the architect's sister-in-law, the house occupied a narrow plot that backed into sheer granite cliffs and consisted of little more than a pair of whitewashed concrete slabs embedded in the hillside and a spiral staircase that ascended the escarpment to a tiny coda of a room with expansive views over Ipanema and the Atlantic. The house remained, at the time, in the hands of the original owner's daughter, an architect, who had carefully preserved its original layout but had never had the funds to invest in renovations or upkeep. The floors were covered in cheap terra-cotta slabs slicked with

In the living room, antique Cappadocian saddle pads
lend warmth and shape to the space's minimalist lines.

shiny black paint, and a small interior patio was enclosed like a terrarium behind glass panels that opened only at the top. The downstairs bedrooms were damp and dark, and the spiral staircase—the only flourish reminiscent of Niemeyer's famous love for curves—had been wrapped in tall glass panels, turning it into a pneumatic tube. The room at the top, its windows broken, had been all but abandoned.

By the time Varejão and Buarque saw the house, it had been on the market for several years. Previous potential buyers had proposed turning the bedrooms into a garage and adding a second story, a plan that would have obliterated Niemeyer's subtle, if imperfect, plans. Others had wanted to demolish the house completely. Despite its lofty provenance, the house, like so many modernist works around the world, enjoyed no heritage protections. "It's very common in Brazil to buy something like this and tear it down," says Varejão, whose diverse work often deals with the cruelties and erasures of Brazilian history. "The owner was desperate to sell to people who understood its value."

Both natives of Rio, Varejão and Buarque understood that value well. "The landscape is such an important part of living in Rio," Varejão says. "When I was a teenager, I would count the days that I *didn't* go to the beach." When she and Buarque decided to buy a house, "we preferred to live in a city house that was *also* a weekend house, rather than do what people have to do in São Paulo"—Brazil's biggest city, with a population of more than twenty million—"and battle your way out of the city on a Friday just to get some air," she says. "In Rio, you have all of that *within* the city." In the Niemeyer house, which, unlike its bulky, terra-cotta-roofed neighbors, deferred so gracefully to its surroundings, they would have that nature quite literally in their backyard. "We saw how much we could improve

on what was there," Buarque says, "because, ultimately, the project is *amazing.*"

Over the course of five years, Varejão and Buarque dramatically restructured the house without visibly transforming Niemeyer's original project. In the first stage, conceived and executed with architect Rodrigo Cerviño López and landscape architect Isabel Duprat, they excavated a garage beneath the structure and turned the driveway into a staircase paved in gray Brazilian soapstone laced with white veins, a herculean effort that allowed them to transform the carport into a garden and to open windows across the house's rear. Inside, they replaced the static windows around the patio with sliding doors that connect the living and dining areas through a tropical tableau of ferns, palms, and philodendrons.

About eighteen months into the project, the couple bought the lot next door in order to demolish the hulking four-story mansion that loomed over their property. Working from this point on with Duprat and Rio-based architect Lia Siqueira, they opened the second lot to create a garden, a pool lined with the same dramatic Brazilian soapstone, and a partially enclosed living area, the roof of which doubled as a paved terrace at the house's entry level. That terrace offered an entirely new perspective on the house's simple, rationalist form and onto the soaring granite altar of Corcovado Hill, far beyond.

To bring all that greenery inside, they cut a circular porthole window into the living room—a detail borrowed from another Niemeyer house, farther down the Atlantic coast. They stripped the glass panels from the spiral staircase and wrapped it in a ribbon of whitewashed metal. Sunlight and nature now filter in from all sides. "Almost all the changes we made were removing things," says Varejão. "All we added was transparency."

Since moving to the house in 2016, Varejão and Buarque have felt their native city's connection to its habitat more profoundly than ever. Hummingbirds and toucans and patrols of capuchin monkeys descend from the mountains to explore Duprat's gardens. Varejão takes regular weekend hikes with her teenage daughter, passing from the city to the forest in mere moments and arriving at dazzling waterfalls and plunge pools in less than an hour. "It's a paradise," Buarque says of his home and, by extension, of his city, a place known to many as the Cidade Maravilhosa—"the Marvelous City."

Spoken here, among so much beauty, those words read not as a prideful assertion but as a modest statement of historical fact. Though they have been reduced, through the years, to a visual cliché, a romantic shorthand for Rio's effortless sensuality, the mountains here—from the distant peak of Tijuca to the tilting twins of the Two Brothers at the far end of Ipanema—are more than just a stage set for the city that lives among them. They are its heart.

An internal garden of palms, ferns, and philodendrons rises through the center of the house, providing a lush backdrop to a trio of loop chairs by Swiss industrial designer Willy Guhl.

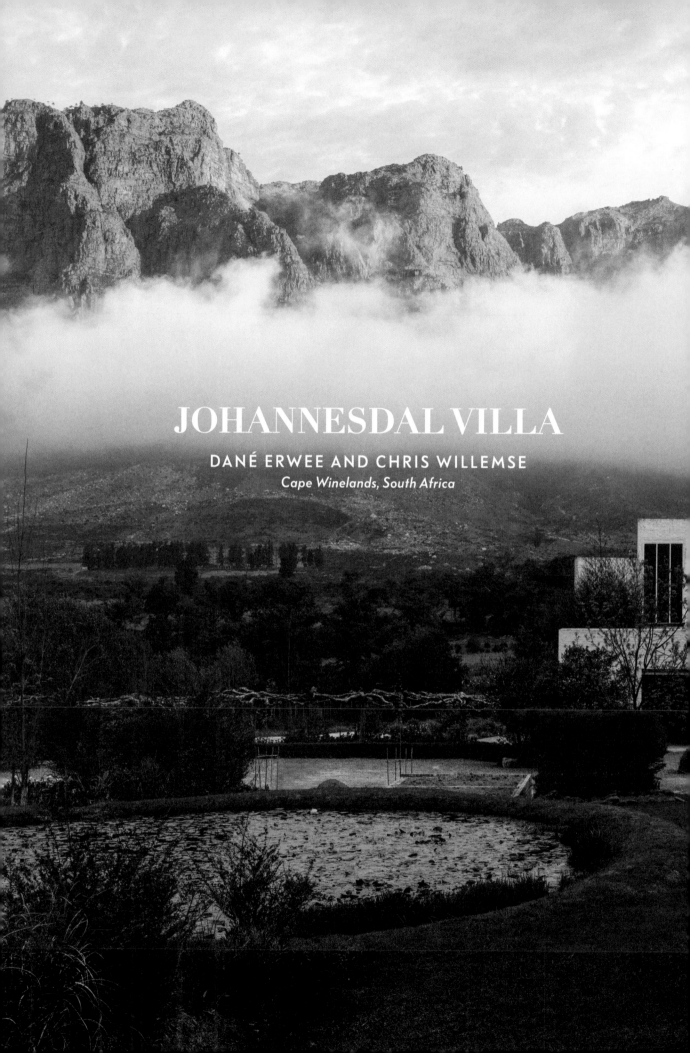

JOHANNESDAL VILLA

DANÉ ERWEE AND CHRIS WILLEMSE
Cape Winelands, South Africa

ON SUMMER EVENINGS, AS THE SUN passes west over the southern edge of the African continent, the jagged face of Drakenstein Mountain catches fire, its craggy limestone surface flushing pale pink and then a dazzling, incandescent red before fading into darkness like a lantern snuffed out. Living barely a mile from the mountain's foot, "you get into nasty habits," quips floral designer and flower farmer Dané Erwee, who, in 2007, built a modern farmhouse here with his partner, Chris Willemse. "You sit on the stoop and watch the mountains. When it catches the reflection right, the swimming pool becomes a pot of gold," he says. "It just paralyzes you, it's that beautiful."

In the late 1990s, Erwee, who studied landscape architecture, and Willemse, a horticulturist, came to the Cape Winelands, a district of Cape Dutch farmhouses and orderly vineyards slipped between the peaks of the Cape Fold Mountains northeast of Cape Town, South Africa. Not long after, in 1999, the couple opened a flower shop in town called OKASIE, a business that has since expanded to include events and elaborate installations, like sculptural wafts of cream and mauve roses or delicate white clusters of mock orange suspended overhead like constellations. That year, and entirely by accident, they came across the property where they would eventually build their home. "We just stumbled upon this piece of land, and five days later, we bought it," Erwee recalls. "We became obsessed."

From the start, their intention was to live on and farm the land. Situated between the towering bookends of the Drakenstein and Simonsberg mountains, the six-acre plot was largely protected from the fierce winds that often whip through the Western Cape region. Sheltered by the surrounding highlands, the land had "a fabulous climate for flowers," Erwee says. It would, he and Willemse thought, make an ideal nursery to supply OKASIE with the native and exotic plants that, when combined in unexpected ways, have become the business's signature.

The land also came with challenges. Though set along the modest two-lane highway that connects Stellenbosch, an important urban district in the winelands, to the historic town of Franschhoek, the lot had neither electricity nor vehicular access from the street. Before anything, Erwee and Willemse had to deal with the bureaucratic mess of getting on the power grid and building a driveway to connect their future house to the main road. Beyond the practical challenges, the prospect of moving from the secure comforts of the Stellenbosch suburbs to an open patch of land in the country "was overwhelming," Erwee says. "You don't have boundaries. It's just you and your partner and your two dogs." Years passed before the couple was prepared to build.

When the time did come, around 2006, Erwee and Willemse reached out to architect Henri Comrie, who had returned to his native South Africa two years before, following a stint as a student in London and Oxford. They'd met by chance in 1998, at a mutual friend's home, just after Erwee and Willemse had moved to Stellenbosch. At the time, Comrie recalls, "Chris and Dané hinted that, if they ever had to design a house for themselves, they would approach me."

After visiting the couple's home in Stellenbosch, Comrie came up with a design for a shedlike building that sat delicately on the earth. Erwee and Willemse read this first project as an outgrowth of a Cape modern movement that was itself deeply indebted to the local vernacular of Cape Dutch farmhouses, with their white walls and peaked roofs. As Comrie recalls, Erwee, dissatisfied with the first draft, suggested something more abstract. "Then [Comrie] made a severe U-turn and gave us this white, Barragánesque block," says Erwee, who was raised on a vegetable and wheat farm in the rural Western Cape province. The new

project would rise from the plot as a monolithic volume of whitewashed brick (the most common finish and material in the area's traditional buildings) that "reaches upward to mimic the surrounding peaks," Comrie says. "It's solid—it has a hell of a presence," Erwee notes, "but we still managed to get a farmhouse. It has all that nostalgia from my childhood."

Like the houses of Luis Barragán, the celebrated mid-century Mexican architect whose work has exerted a powerful influence over Comrie's approach to building, the villa is, at first, inscrutable. The house reads as a single geometric block, a sculptural object set down between the surrounding peaks.

As one enters the house, its sturdy exterior gives way to a labyrinth of hallways and half stairs. As the space descends over the contours of the lot, floors drop and ceilings rise while the heavy folds of brick at the building's entrance dissolve into exposed ceiling beams and soaring panes of glass at the rear. Those material and spatial transformations guide visitors from the close intimacy of the entryway to an airy parlor and dining area connected, through floor-to-ceiling windows, to an open-air living room that offers cinematic views toward the flower farm and the sheer cliffs of Drakenstein.

Maximalists by nature, Erwee and Willemse softened the house's hard lines by filling it with antique furniture and textiles, landscapes and portraits painted by Erwee, and a mad, marvelous profusion of objects. Ceramics and books crowd the shelves and mantelpieces, atlas pages have become wallpaper, and globes have been transformed into lamps or overflow from a woven basket like a pile of citrus fruit.

As time has passed and the house's surfaces have become worn—doors scratched, paint chipped, stone floors smoothed by footfall—so, too, has the building given itself over

to the garden. Boston ivy, which flushes crimson each fall, has engulfed much of the home's rear wall, originally a matrix of glass and steel framed by white brick, while lilacs, with their dangling clusters of springtime blossoms, have all but invaded the primary bathroom.

Elsewhere, it can be difficult to discern which interventions are natural and which have been carefully crafted by Erwee and Willemse. Porcelain calla lilies mounted on copper wire wrap around a denuded branch of ivy that snakes across the patio. Flowers blossom in the textiles on throw pillows and climb over the surface of time-worn carpets. And in the foyer, live orchids and a potted fiddle-leaf fig blend into a canvas (painted by Erwee) that depicts the fan-like leaves of elephant ear Colocasia.

This slippage between the man-made and natural extends into the garden, which, like the house, is in a constant state of transformation. Toward the back of the lot, traversed by a narrow river, neat rows of hydrangeas grow under shade trees, and roses blossom in full sun. Closer to the house, the garden grows wilder, abundant

with shrubs and arbors. Depending on the season, Erwee will forage branches frosted with pale pink crab apple blossoms or raid the high branches of tulip trees for their green, cup-shaped blossoms. At a recent wedding reception held at Johannesdal 1207, the venue Erwee and Willemse opened next door to the house in 2020, branches from a mulberry tree were stripped of their leaves to make a graphic composition of bare branches and lurid fruit beneath a corona of orchids and roses. "These are the things you can achieve only if you live with these plants, if you really *know* them," Erwee says. "I like that playfulness, that you can manipulate nature, that it can become art."

In recent years, Erwee has become more invested in pursuing his painting, less excited about the ephemeral making of occasion—that's Willemse's area—and "more passionate about the growing and the farming," he says, "the longer-term project of seeing things mature." That sort of transformation is, after all, the foundational fact of landscapes both cultivated and wild, of making art and of making a home.

OPPOSITE, LEFT: In the entry hall, potted orchids growing in front of a canvas of soaring taro leaves.

OPPOSITE, RIGHT: A wall of botanical drawings by Erwee take their inspiration from the nineteenth-century French botanist Pierre-Joseph Redouté.

Lustrous brass panels make a sumptuous headboard in the house's primary bedroom.

OPPOSITE: A profusion of objects fills every space in the house, like a domestic Wunderkammer. In the entry hall, a plywood banister, now painted a vibrant shade of green, was a later addition.

The seating area on the second-floor verandah with a stool, hand-upholstered by Erwee, and a vitrine crowded with keepsakes and mementos from the couple's travels.

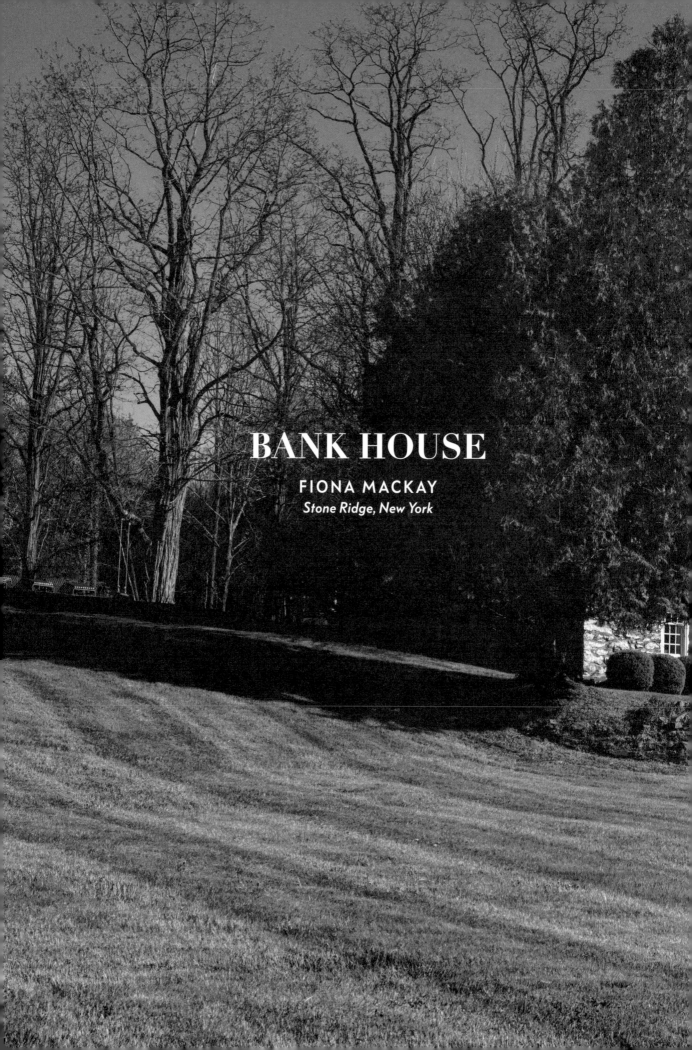

BANK HOUSE

FIONA MACKAY
Stone Ridge, New York

BEFORE MOVING TO NEW YORK IN 2014 and eventually purchasing a Colonial stone house in the Catskill Mountains, art adviser Fiona Mackay spent countless weekends of her youth hiking up Table Mountain, the iconic mesa that looms over her native city of Cape Town, South Africa. The mountain's landscape was both lunar and lush, its rocky trails lined by towering shrubs of proteas, their Paleocene blossoms like exploding stars. The mountain shaped not only the climate of Mackay's hometown, but also her relationship to the idea of home. The mountain, she says, "has a powerful presence in the memory of anyone who grew up in Cape Town, especially those of us who moved away."

Mackay first left home at seventeen for an internship at *Vogue* in London and, after returning home for her undergraduate studies, spent time living, working, and studying in both London and Paris before moving to New York to pursue a business degree at Columbia University.

She loved all three cities for their access to endless culture, their cosmopolitanism, and their energy, but she missed the beauty and slower pace of home, the connection to the soaring mountains and the endless South Atlantic—the freedom of "being in a place," she says, "where it is enough to simply do nothing and enjoy the beauty of your surroundings."

Mackay gave birth to her son in early 2016 and immediately felt her innate need for space come rushing back. "Raising a child in a tiny Brooklyn apartment seemed untenable," she says, and so she and her partner at the time went looking for a house in the country. Friends from the city had recently bought a house in the village of Accord, New York, a minuscule hamlet in the Catskills, which rise gently to the west of the Hudson River. While visiting them on a summer weekend in 2016, Mackay went out for a drive along a narrow country road. Golden-hour sunshine glinted off a burbling stream. "There's something magical about the

Rather than reupholstering the Napoleon III armchairs that she found at a Massachusetts antiques market, Mackay chose to leave the pieces' calico lining exposed, revealing their architectural forms.

light around there at that time of year and at that time of day," she says. She fell in love and started looking for a home, eventually finding an eighteenth-century farmhouse in the village of Stone Ridge, north of the steep sandstone cliff faces of the Shawangunk Mountains. Within two months, she'd negotiated the purchase of the house.

As luck would have it, the previous owners had invested heavily, installing central air, modern plumbing, and new electrical lines. "The house is really quite simple, so there's not much to do in terms of layout—I mean, the downstairs walls are two feet thick," Mackay says. "We really just had to give it a fresh lick of paint and change the lighting and furniture."

Today, each of the house's three floors— from its cavelike entry level embedded in the hillside to an airy top floor added by the previous owners—generates a world and atmosphere of its own. Downstairs, rustic white plaster coats the walls, which in turn support ax-hewn ceiling beams nine feet overhead. Here, Mackay filled the space with furniture that leans toward a deconstructed historicism. For a pair of antique Napoleon III armchairs found at the Brimfield antique market in Massachusetts, she chose to leave their bone-colored calico lining exposed, as on a seamstress's dummy. In the dining room, classic Windsor chairs frame a reclaimed-wood dining table in a delicate fence of spindles. Above the table, a pair of small canvases swim among gentle waves of plaster. One of the works is by local outsider artist Earl Swanigan, who died in 2019; the other, of a crayon-bright poodle, drawn in purple and green expressionist brushstrokes by South African artist Georgina Gratrix.

One flight up, the density and weight of the ground floor loosens as light and space slip between cracks in the aged materials. Set down in 1758, when the house was built, the floorboards are held together not with sturdy tongue-and-groove joints—a technique not invented until the following century—but with centuries-old nails. Through hundreds of frigid winters and hot, damp summers, those boards have warped and pulled apart. "You can see the downstairs through the spaces between the boards, which is *wonderful*," Mackay says. "It was one of the things that attracted us to the house." Rather than furnishings that gestured toward the house's late Colonial origins, here Mackay combined mid-century classics, clean and utilitarian, with luxurious linens, a fascination since her time at Karu, a homewares brand focused on handmade items from India and South Africa that she co-founded in 2017. The uppermost floor she left blank. "The rest of the house is so textural and full of history— there's literally centuries-old dust between the floorboards—so this space is, for me, more calming," she says.

If the house is a study in textures and moods, a place of respite from the cramped city, then the nineteenth-century barn at the far end of the four-acre property is dedicated to cultivating community among artists and craftspeople. Though Mackay had found the house itself in good shape, the barn required a full renovation to become usable space. After clearing out the hydroponic irrigation system and the rusted-out axes that previous owners had left to accumulate in the barn's cobwebbed corners, Mackay transformed the space into a studio and white-cube gallery for exhibiting works from Tiwa Select, the LA-based craft and utilitarian-art gallery with which she's been associated since 2021. It has served, too, as an informal residency for artists like Gratrix, Broderick Shoemaker, and the Tiwa-associated textile creator Megumi Shauna Arai, who, at the time of her stay, had been working from a minuscule New York City apartment where

OPPOSITE: In the summer, Mackay fills the sink with ice and bottles of wine to serve in the sunroom. The white vessel is by South African potter Jade Paton.

The first thing Mackay does each morning is take her English bulldog, Petal, out to the yard. "Starting your day by putting your bare feet on grass is a very special feeling," she says.

she had to lay her work out on her bed in order to see it in its entirety. "Being able to offer this space to her to use," Mackay recalls, "just felt so valuable."

Space, in Mackay's universe, has nothing to do with isolation but, rather, with possibilities—for creativity, for community, for perspective. Though winter is quiet here, in the summer, Mackay hosts guests on the weekends and throws dinner parties in the woods. ("It's a really magical place to have a meal—if you can manage to put out enough repellent for the mosquitos," she jokes.) Each year at midsummer, when fireflies spangle the darkness, friends come in from far and wide for music and dancing into the early hours of the morning.

The house has encouraged Mackay to think on a different timescale than cities like London or Paris allow. "Being here, in a place that was built with such care, with materials that have lasted for hundreds of years, starts to make you think in terms of longevity and circular economies and even heirlooms," she says. "I buy a piece of furniture now, and I think, 'This could belong to my child someday.'" Living among mountains situates you not only in the span of seconds, minutes, and hours, but also in the geological span of centuries, millennia, and eons—stretches of time in which transformation is not only possible, but inevitable.

For Mackay, the city is still home, and creating connections between people and places is still her primary passion. (Her most recent project, Kombi, is a New York City–based platform for artists and designers from South Africa.) Having grown up among mountains, Mackay understands that open landscapes and quiet rooms can do much more than provide solitude. "Buying this house really allowed my soul to breathe," she says. "There's something about empty space that allows you to dream."

On the house's airy second floor, Mackay's interiors lean away from the deconstructed historicism of the ground floor, focusing instead on fine textiles and simple, honest furnishings from a range of periods and styles, like this ceramic bedside table by Natalie Gehrels.

OPPOSITE: Elsewhere on the property, Mackay transformed a disused nineteenth-century barn into a white-box gallery and studio space, which she has lent out to friends and colleagues like the New York–based textile artist Megumi Shauna Arai.

HOME IN THE ENGADIN

NOT VITAL
Sent, Switzerland

The stüva—the traditional heart of every Engadin home, where families gather—furnished with an antique table of local manufacture and an original Bidermeier buffet.

ON A WINTER MORNING IN 1951, when Swiss artist Not Vital was three years old, he and his older brother went out into the yard of the family home in the village of Sent to build a tunnel beneath a thick mantle of snow. A short time later, Vital's brother was sent off to school, but Not stayed put, intoxicated by the bright, clean scent of the air and by the luminous mountain sun refracted through compacted snow. "It wasn't so comfortable to be in that tunnel, of course. It would have been more comfortable to go back inside, to my parents' home," Vital says now. "But I thought at that moment, 'This is my habitat. This is *my house.*'"

For nearly twenty years, the meaning of that elemental word has been at the heart of Vital's artistic practice. In 2005, he built his House to Watch the Sunset outside the desert city of Agadez, in Niger, a forty-three-foot tower of mud, straw, and dung conceived with the sole purpose of observing the spectacular Saharan sky. He repeated the structure a decade later in the depths of the Amazon, this time using local timber; and again in Switzerland, using concrete. (A version in aluminum will soon be installed on the island of Tonga, with another planned for the windswept plains of Mongolia.) He adapted the idea in 2017 for the House to Watch Three Volcanoes, on a remote island in eastern Indonesia, building a stark white observatory with an interior lined in bamboo and straw, the materials used in the traditional houses of the surrounding countryside. In 2008, Vital bought an island of solid marble in the middle of an icy lake in Chilean Patagonia and started excavating what would become a 180-foot tunnel to make a shelter not unlike that magical habitat of his early memories.

All these are "houses" only in that childlike sense—spaces, as Vital puts it, where "you can stay." Vital has lived in more-conventional homes in Paris, Rome, Lucca, New York, Beijing, and, most recently, Rio de Janeiro. Yet, for all that nomadism, he has always returned home

When Vital bought back the half of the family home that had been left to his brother, he immediately set to work restoring the building to how it was during his childhood.

OPPOSITE: In the dining room, a 2016 landscape by Vital in marble and plaster erupts from the wall above an antique Chinese chair and a Cy Twombly lithograph from 1984.

A marble bath stands at the center of the primary bathroom to better take in mountain views just outside.

OPPOSITE: An original fireplace off the dining room.

When Vital restored the house, he removed the glass panels that had been added to the summer verandah and opened it directly to the elements; in winter, snowdrifts often fill the semi-enclosed room.

to Sent and to the majestic Alpine landscapes of eastern Switzerland's Engadin Valley.

A tourist destination since the nineteenth century, the Engadin is also a place of migrations. Many of the valley's natives, Vital says, spent winters running coffeehouses in Italy and would build their expansive stone-and-plaster Engadin houses from money earned abroad. (They were known locally as "swallows.") "Going away is not new, so I was very young when I decided that that was what I was going to do."

At age fourteen, Vital left home for high school and never lived full time in Sent again, yet he's never gone for more than eight months without at least a visit to the village of his birth. "If you're from this valley, you always tend to come back here," he says. "Nature, the surroundings, the language—we speak Romansh, a language that not even one percent of the Swiss population speaks, so I had to come back to use my mother tongue." Today, Vital's properties in the valley include a sculpture park at the edge of Sent, a house for his foundation in the nearby village of Ardez, and an eleventh-century castle on a hilltop roughly halfway between the two. But the family home has always been his touchstone.

The house entered Vital's family in 1946, when his father, who earned a comfortable living in the timber industry, purchased it from one of Sent's swallows, who'd renovated the building in 1920 and turned its old barn, now Vital's studio, into a dance hall. Vital's own family had houses closer to the village's compact center, but his mother dreamed of open space and expansive views. "She always said that the day they moved into the house, May 1, 1946, was the most beautiful day of her life," Vital says. "She died there, too, at one hundred years old." Afterward, Vital and his brother inherited the house together, adjusting the property to

accommodate separate apartments for them both. In 2019, Vital bought his brother's half of the house. "That same day, I started to change it back to how it used to be," he says. "I wanted the house I remembered from my childhood."

He tore out a second kitchen and demolished the walls that had enclosed the summer verandah, leaving its carved pine arches open to the elements. In the summer, he hosts dinner parties for friends from around the world; during winter storms, the room—as exposed to the elements as the watchtowers in the Amazon and the Sahara—fills with snow. On any given day, Vital says, he has no idea where he might sleep—in the castle, in Ardez, or in one of the several bedrooms in the house at Sent. (He has never counted the house's rooms, he says, and wouldn't know where to begin: "What's a room? Everything that has a door?") Even in Sent, he says, he often moves between bedrooms over the course of a night. "I start in one; I move to another at three in the morning," he says. "When you wake up, it means it's time to move on." Vital is a nomad even at home.

The house in Sent, finally, is both homage and home, a romance for the valley whose gravitational force is also, paradoxically, the very thing that allowed Vital to roam so widely. Isolated from the world, the Engadin is both the periphery and, at least for Vital, the center. "You look one way, people speak German; look another, and they speak Italian—it's a different country and a different language. The Engadin stops, and it's completely different," he says. From the verandah, the mountains rear up to block the horizon, a vertiginous barrier between here and everywhere else. But Vital still nurtures a child's sense of possibility and wonder. "From here," he says, "I can see over the mountain to a different life."

In his mother's former bedroom, Vital restored the original pine wall panels, a typical element of traditional architecture in the Engadin Valley.

The dining room of Vital's home in Sent, Switzerland.

There is a saying in Romansh, Vital's mother tongue, spoken as a first language by fewer than 50,000 people: "If God lived on earth," the saying goes, "he would live in the Engadin."

MINIWAWA

CHRISTIANA MAVROMATIS AND SCOTT ARNOLD
Onteora Park, New York

CHRISTIANA MAVROMATIS AND HER husband, Scott Arnold, first laid eyes on what would become their summer house in New York's Catskill Mountains on a frigid day in April. Snow covered the front lawn—in the summer, it is a thick sponge of damp green moss—and sap trickled slowly from the tapped maple trees lining the driveway. Mavromatis and Arnold had driven from their home in Park Slope, Brooklyn, more or less on a whim, curious to see the sprawling mansion they'd stumbled upon while looking at upstate properties that called for a renovation. Neither took the prospect seriously. "We're not people who buy this kind of house; it was ridiculous," Mavromatis says. "But from the moment we drove in, it felt magical."

The drive from New York City took less than three hours, with the last sixteen miles or so climbing nineteen hundred feet into the hills, where temperatures are regularly fifteen degrees cooler than they are at sea level. Built as an inn at the end of the nineteenth century and then converted into a private home in the first years of the twentieth, the house had never been winterized. Inside, it was freezing and totally undisturbed, as though the chilly spring air had slowed time itself. Newspapers covered the mattresses in the seven bedrooms. (The original structure's third floor, where the majority of the inn's guests would have stayed, was removed sometime in the mid-twentieth century.) Stacks of linens filled the closets. Powder dusted the tops of bureaus. Boxes of photos and onionskin telegrams offered glimpses into the house's past. "There's a whole family tree for this house that goes back a hundred thirty years," Arnold says. "We just drew ourselves in."

That family tree has its roots in an artists' colony called Onteora, founded in 1887 by textile designer Candace Wheeler, who was then at the height of her eventful career in New York City, and her brother Francis Thurber. In its early years, Onteora hosted writers, artists,

Originally built as an inn to serve the community at Onteora, the house had a third floor that was removed sometime in the twentieth century. Currently, the home has seven bedrooms on its second floor.

and thinkers like Mark Twain, painter George Bellows, and conservationist John Burroughs—visitors who would make the trek from the city into the virtually undisturbed wilderness of the Catskills to camp out under the stars. Built to house early guests at Onteora, Mavromatis and Arnold's house has always played a part in the community at large, which today consists of some sixty-five families. "I heard stories from people that they learned how to ride a bike in the ballroom on rainy days and from older gentlemen whose first job was to rake leaves in the yard," Mavromatis says, "so it really feels like we're stewards of that legacy."

After purchasing the house, Arnold and Mavromatis dove into renovations, always with the aim of respecting the historical integrity of the house and its surroundings. Sunlight and snow slipped through gaps in the hemlock-bark shingles that sheathed the house's half-rotten exterior. In the ballroom, on the ground floor, they found remarkably well-preserved wainscoting and walls covered in the tattered remains of hemp linen, used in the late nineteenth century as a packing material for importing furniture from Europe and frequently repurposed as a wallcovering; when they recovered the walls, Mavromatis and Arnold approximated the texture of that material as closely as they could. Arnold, who laid wooden floors in Texas as a college student, spent hours sanding and staining the ceiling—"It's my Sistine Chapel," he jokes—and scouting antique fixtures in Tannersville, the nearest town. Using period-appropriate fabrics, they restored the moth-eaten furnishings they found in the house, many of them covered in oil cloth and dust.

Together, Arnold and Mavromatis perused a treasure trove of Kodachrome prints and documents that told stories both hopeful and tragic: military discharge records and checkbook stubs, letters of congratulation for a marriage, and a baby book whose abridged entries suggest an unthinkable loss. "It's not some fairy tale. There are trials and tribulations, celebrations and mourning," Arnold says. "It's real life." The design today, with its color palette of cream and ochre, its stone walls and rustic tables, and its rocking chairs with woven-cane seats, suggests not just the memories Arnold and Mavromatis hope to make for their family, but also a deep love for the stories they've uncovered in the process.

For Mavromatis, Arnold, and their two children, the house in the Catskills has become far more than a place to pass long summer weekends. On the way in, they invariably roll down the windows at the top of the mountain to breathe cool mist off a waterfall that rushes out of the hills—a first taste of an alternative universe. During the long days of June and July, the family will host dinner parties for visiting friends or picnic by the lake. They spend days hiking and canoeing or watching the deer, foxes, and, on occasion, bears that wander across their fern-garlanded yard. "There's always a project. Stacking wood, which is a full-day activity, and planting flower bulbs in the garden," Mavromatis says.

This free and active way of life is an important part of what drew the couple to such an ambitious project, one that required a degree of commitment and will for which not even their gut renovation of their Park Slope townhouse in 2010 could truly prepare them. More than just a project to satisfy their own creative urges, the house was a powerful lesson to impart to their children about work: "We wanted to show them that it's worthwhile to be bold, strike out, be creative, and back that up with really, really hard work. That if you do all that, you can build something beautiful," Arnold says. "You can call it foolhardy or you can call it romantic." Or, perhaps foolhardy and romantic are, in the end, one and the same.

OPPOSITE: Arnold hand-finished the house's wooden ceilings like those in the house's dining room, pictured here, often spending eleven hours at a stretch on his back. "It's my Sistine Chapel," he jokes.

In restoring textiles and wallcoverings, Mavromatis and Arnold sought out patterns that recalled those by the designer Candace Wheeler, who co-founded Onteora at the height of her eventful New York career.

Dried flowers from the garden stand on an antique table in one of the bedrooms.

OPPOSITE: A pair of vintage leather chairs flank a carpet that Mavromatis's mother purchased on a trip to England.

MINIWAWA

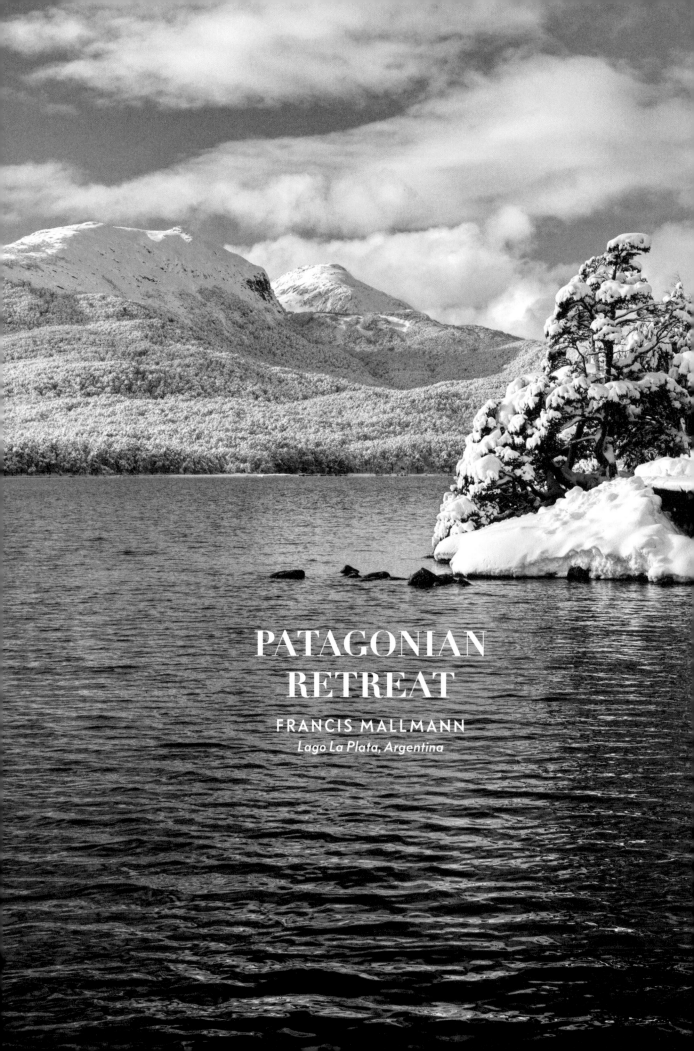

PATAGONIAN RETREAT

FRANCIS MALLMANN
Lago La Plata, Argentina

PREVIOUS PAGES: Clad in black metal siding, the guesthouses on Mallmann's island, originally built as film sets for his many television cooking programs before being relocated to the far edge of Patagonia, stand like shadows in the snow.

In the dining room, Zalto stemware shares shelf space with Bernardaud china. Chairs originally used at one of Mallmann's eleven restaurants circle a table covered by a leather tablecloth that Mallmann stitched together himself.

IN ANOTHER LIFE, THE CELEBRATED Argentine chef Francis Mallmann would have loved to work as a couturier. Textiles are everywhere in the cluster of cabins he built to welcome guests at his remote island hideaway on the mountainous border with Chile: Reams of French linen crowd into his closet, woolen shawls hang on hooks in the entry hall, and Italian cotton sheets sheath the cloud-soft beds. In the spare-yet-luxurious dining room of the main cabin, long knives of sunlight reflecting off the blizzard-white landscape cut across a leather table cover the color of *dulce de leche* that he stitched together himself. Everything in that quietly elegant room was handpicked by Mallmann as well. The Zalto stemware, delicate as spiderwebs, crowded onto shelves alongside Bernardaud china scrolled with cobalt flowers; the jars of lapsang souchong, a black tea redolent of gun smoke; and whole-grain Colombian coffee lined up on the cypress countertops at the far end of the room—together, they express

the notorious love for beauty that has, for decades, driven his expansive (and, at times, confounding) approach to love, work, and family. "You can't embrace everything in life," he says with a smirk both melancholic and wry. "But the dream is always there."

Few people have come closer to that dream than Mallmann. At sixty-seven, he has published seven cookbooks, decorated a dozen houses, and, from 1983 to 2013, appeared weekly on televised cooking shows. He collects volumes of poetry, antique carpets, and contemporary art. He paints watercolors, plays guitar, sews, and arranges flowers. He travels constantly among his eleven restaurants on three continents and his six homes scattered about Patagonia, Uruguay, and the South of France, conjuring spare time from the dark hours of early morning to pore over films by Visconti, Fellini, or Kieślowski.

Mallmann's love for food, the most prominent of his many passions, started in his childhood home in Bariloche, a resort town in

On the mainland a short distance from the island, Mallmann's team sets up lunch service at a clearing near a glacial stream flowing fast and clear out of the woods and toward the water.

northern Patagonia, where he says, "Teatime was a religious thing," and where his mother would host parties for musicians, biologists, and mathematicians, invited to the edge of the world by his father's postgraduate foundation at the local university. Mallmann's love for restaurants began in Bariloche, too, at a bistro run by a German baron and his wife. "I remember the first time I went, when I was eight or nine," he recalls. "It was under a tree, and the tables were outside. It really shocked me, these tables and tablecloths, the music and the shade. The food—I can't remember anything—but the *setting*," he says. "I think I went into restaurants more for the décor than the food."

Mallmann first came to the mountain-fringed shores of Lago La Plata in 1986. Having heard of the lake's extravagant beauty, he and a friend set up camp on a fifteen-acre island near its western extreme, to protect themselves from roving cows that wandered across the border from Chile, just over the adjacent ridge. Two years later, Mallmann started importing timber from Bariloche—there are no logging permits to be had this far south in Patagonia—which he used to assemble a simple cabin. It took five years to complete. "The day I had a shower there with hot water, I just cried," he says. "I couldn't believe it."

For thirty years, the island served as a reprieve from the increasingly relentless pace of his professional life and as a space where he could bring together his ever-growing family. (Today, he has seven children, ages four to forty-one, with four different women.) After the success of the first season of the Netflix series *Chef's Table* in 2015, Mallmann, who'd filmed the bulk of his episode on the island, started receiving requests for visits and workshops. Restless as ever, he opened his refuge to guests in 2017, having imported cabins originally built as stage sets for his television shows and

reassembled them at the water's edge. Cloaked in black corrugated metal, the cabins stand like shadows in a snowstorm, their whitewashed interiors both sumptuous and raw. Axes hang in the entry hall. In the winter, oversize couches in the living room, made for enjoying books and tea and whiskey, combat the constant chill leaking through picture windows that frame the lake and mountains.

A year later, he built his own studio and living quarters over the dock. This is where visitors arrive after a journey that begins with a flight from Buenos Aires to the grim seaside oil town of Comodoro Rivadavia; continues with a six-hour drive west across the flat, rugged expanse of the Patagonian flatlands; and ends with another, hour-long journey by boat over the shimmering surface of Lago La Plata, which snakes between the snowcapped peaks of the Andes.

Mallmann's rooms are a shrine to his countless aesthetic pursuits. A desk stretches the length of the western wall, where books by John Muir, William Blake, Karl Marx, and Clarice Lispector share shelf space with monographs on Nan Goldin, Emilio Pucci, Eugène Delacroix, and the indigenous peoples of the Tierra del Fuego. Pale pink eyeglasses nestle in a basket of fabric swatches from Liberty of London, and pastels are scattered over a ceramic plate stained with watercolors. In the kitchen, Jeroboams (aka double magnums) of cognac and Chartreuse stand alongside English china in vivid canary yellow, translucent as sunshine. Antique wool blankets, their floral patterns introduced to the interior province of Santiago del Estero by English railroad builders in the nineteenth century, drape the floors. Other blankets slouch over the backs of rustic wooden benches in the open-air kitchen and dining room, contained within a structure that consists of little more than two wooden walls

Antique throws lend warmth to an open-sided shed
where Mallmann serves lunch.

Before opening the island to visitors, Mallmann spent thirty years visiting exclusively with family and friends. In that time he built a wooden cabin and a handful of other simple structures, like the woodshed pictured here.

The bathroom in Mallmann's apartments, perched over the dock where guests arrive, includes a massive block of soap, a tub for soaking, and curtains made from ochre linen.

and a roof, an open fire, and a superlative mountain view.

And then there is the food: the onions and beets and sweet potatoes pulled hot from the coals; the sliced polenta seared on an open brazier; the so-called welcome cake, a ham-and-cheese tart blanketed in a crumbly olive oil batter, beaten eggs, and a dusting of sugar that Mallmann adapted from a recipe from his grandmother's short-lived Montevideo teahouse. But cooking is no more the central point here than the houses themselves. Together, they form part of the relentlessly elegant (and occasionally chaotic) *Gesamtkunstwerk*—the term coined by Wagner to define the "complete work of art" of his outrageously ambitious operas—that has been Mallmann's life, a gift he can both bestow and control.

Developed over so many years in a landscape Mallmann knows intimately, the island is the zenith of that work, a place of communion that brings together all his many loves—people and places, flavors and scents and textures—under a canopy of native lenga, coihue, and nire trees. It is also, perhaps, the purest expression of the "silent language" that he says defined his Andean upbringing, "this communication with the geography, the lakes, the rivers, the wind, the sun, the snow, the forest." Elusive and wide-ranging, it is the impatient mother tongue of constant transformation that defines both nature and all creative pursuits. "It's like cooking," he says, as if to explain, then shrugs and smiles, disinclined to translate. "It's a mystery."

Textiles and decor have been an obsession of Mallmann's for much of his life, as evidenced by the profusion of patterns and colors on display in one of the house's guest rooms.

CASA LUNA

MAURICIO PEZO AND SOFÍA VON ELLRICHSHAUSEN
Yungay, Chile

FOR ABOUT A YEAR AND A HALF, BEGINning in 2020, when much of the world had locked down in the face of a global pandemic, architects Mauricio Pezo and Sofía von Ellrichshausen set out to build a world of their own.

Each morning, they would step out of their uninsulated plywood hut—a temporary shelter on their 272-acre lot in the foothills of the Chilean Andes—and scrawl instructions on a chalkboard, indicating to their team which part of their sprawling home-and-studio compound they would build that day. They might draw an L-shaped block with dimensions marked out or sketch a haphazard spiral split into wedges, a staircase reduced to its elemental shape.

Working from those rudimentary diagrams, the builders would erect wooden forms to be filled with rough, expressive concrete. The chalkboard "was like the ones that they put up at village shops and grocery stores to say, *Hay Pan*"—"There's bread"—says von Ellrichshausen, who grew up outside the mountain town of Bariloche at the northern edge of Argentine Patagonia. The construction, in the end, was "not even vernacular, because vernacular requires skill, vocation, artisanship," Pezo says. "Here there's no craft but primitive skills."

Gradually Pezo and von Ellrichshausen and their team—most of them from the same local family who'd returned to their village when city jobs evaporated under strict lockdown conditions—pieced together twelve linked structures that inscribed a square, 246 feet on each side, over the sloped terrain. An asymmetrical cross of both habitable and transitory spaces divided the open center into four courtyards occupied, respectively, by fruit trees, a circular lagoon shaded by willows, a narrow canal like a water feature from a Mughal garden, and a half-wild flower bed that, in springtime, blossoms with spikes of lavender and bright orange poppies. In all, the project, called Casa Luna, or "Moon House," would encompass an area comparable to that of a city block and would contain the

OPPOSITE: In the house's habitable interior spaces, like this meeting room in the studio wing of the complex, the architects covered a layer of insulation with the battered wooden slats originally used as formworks during the project's construction.

Massive square windows throughout the house bring in the surrounding greenery, like the fruit trees that Pezo and von Ellrichshausen surveyed and mapped before they began conceptualizing the project.

Sling chairs designed by the architects are used throughout the compound, including here in the studio's sun-washed meeting room.

The dining table in the architects' home stands alongside a spiral stair contained in a concrete tube, leading to a lofted bedroom above.

couple's home and offices; a gallery and a sewing room; studios for painting, modeling, woodworking, and drawing; three apartments for visiting collaborators; and at least a dozen interstitial spaces with no clear use at all.

Typical of the work the couple has done since founding their firm, Pezo von Ellrichshausen, in 2002, Casa Luna would be both monumental and modest, its runic perforations open to the forest and sky, its interiors clad in wood recycled from construction and covered with slapdash coats of paint. Built on a former subsistence farm separated from the nearest village by roughly twenty miles of gravel roads—"The expression in Chile," says Pezo, who grew up outside the coastal city of Concepción, seventy-eight miles to the west, "is *Donde el diablo perdió el poncho*" or, "Where the devil lost his poncho"—the house would be imperfect by necessity. Casa Luna, the architects have said, "was born old."

For two years after closing on the purchase of their lot in 2016, Pezo and von Ellrichshausen left it to sit. (Starting in November 2018, they worked in fits and starts with contractors, eventually taking over as builders a year later and starting heavy construction in 2020.) One of the two brothers who had sold them the land continued farming, growing sour cherries, grapes, and *avellanas,* a native variety of chestnut. The architects, who lived at the time in Concepción, visited intermittently. They mapped the stands of fruit trees, pin-straight *raulís* (beeches) and towering *robles* (oaks). In their first winter, they saw how rainwater gathered at a low point in the plot to form the pond that would become a focal point for the largest of the courtyards. Over time, they studied how the seasons inscribed themselves on the land.

Back home in Concepción, the couple developed an ideal program for the compound, assembling lists of the spaces they would need and how

much distance they might want between them. The whole deductive process, the same they use in all their projects, was "the result of questions," von Ellrichshausen says: "How does the sun move? The wind? What do we want close to what? What kind of light do we want where we work?" "The plan," as Pezo puts it, "is a puzzle."

As they answered those questions, the puzzle took shape. The apartments, where roofs could be lower, would sit at the higher end of the lot. The couple's home would sit below, where the 'ten-foot drop in the topography would generate space for a pair of lofted bedrooms beneath the planar roofline. They wanted the space to feel unified without forcing their collaborators, who would come for months-long residencies, to sacrifice their privacy. "We wanted a unitary structure in the landscape," says von Ellrichshausen; the sensation, Pezo adds, of "shared solitude."

As the relationships between spaces coalesced, collateral elements emerged to draw the structure together. A pair of spiral stairs would twist up from the ground floor to the roof, one tightly wound in a concrete tube, the other wrapped loosely around it, the two sharing a starting point and destination but offering radically different experiences of ascent. Soot would slick the walls of an interior fire pit, cloaking them in the penetrating scent of wood smoke and the ritual darkness of a temple bier. A squat, cylindrical library would rest on four cylindrical legs: two containing identical stairways, the other two a toilet and a sink, with four reflective doorways facing one another as in a funhouse's hall of mirrors.

Whole rooms would serve no other purpose than to open around a pre-existing tree, to hold a pair of canvases painted by the architects, to create more pathways into sunbathed courtyards or the banks of fog that sometimes descend over the structure like ghosts.

The walls of an interior firepit are already stained black with soot and permeated with the rich scent of woodsmoke after only a year of use.

OPPOSITE: The play of shadow and light animates the project's otherwise spartan interiors, as in the living room in the guest suite, pictured here.

Unified by its monochromatic materials and repeated geometries, the house in its final form became a celebration, as the architects have said, of "redundancy, monotony, procrastination." It is a provocative repudiation of modernist dogmas of transparency, movement, and efficiency—a maze with many routes to no fixed conclusion. It offers no narratives, no clear entrances or exits, no beginnings or ends, but, instead, the joy of ambiguity, of experience as an end in itself.

Luxury here has little to do with material comfort or impeccably honed details. "More than the quality of construction, it's the volume of air," says Pezo. "Because, in the end," von Ellrichshausen adds, "distance through air becomes time. By expanding distances, you expand time, the resource we all lack." That leap from the primitive to the existential—from the chalkboard in a corner store to the nature of time and space—is, perhaps, the essential fact of the idiosyncratic universe that Pezo and von Ellrichshausen have conjured for themselves here in this distant corner of the world.

Yet despite that distance, Casa Luna is not a temporary retreat from everyday life. Time, here, does not stand still, and the mountains are not a scenic backdrop—they are, in fact, invisible from within the house, hidden away over the wooded horizon. For many, visiting the mountains offers the illusion of escape, the fantasy of connection with the land. But Pezo and von Ellrichshausen are not visitors here, and living in the mountains demands submission to their tectonic timescale. Casa Luna will measure time not just in movement through air or the passage of the sun or the changing of seasons, but in the years that will inscribe themselves on its walls, rudimentary diagrams of the landscape's long life.

The painting studio where Pezo and von Ellrichshausen
work on canvases that range from large-scale
abstractions to fauvist landscapes and carefully
executed elevations for future projects.

The bedroom in one of the three apartments built for the resident architects who come from around the world to work with Pezo and von Ellrichshausen for months at a stretch.

An open gallery separates two of the house's four courtyards.

ACKNOWLEDGMENTS

I feel immensely grateful to everyone who helped in the making of this book, which I am incredibly proud of.

I would like to thank the individual homeowners who graciously opened the doors to their extraordinary refuges. Your warmth, hospitality, and trust allowed us to create a body of work that exceeded my expectations. The creativity and brilliance I saw in each of these homes have inspired me tremendously, and I hope our readers will feel the same. Thank you so much for being a part of this project.

Every image in this book was taken by the incredibly talented Chris Mottalini. Chris, I feel so lucky to have been able to work with you. Thank you for joining me in this project and journey as a true creative partner whose artistry, eye, and talent are unmatched.

All text in this book was written by the brilliant Michael Snyder, whose storytelling brought these houses to life. Thank you for your trust and for your remarkable work.

A tremendous thank-you to Clarkson Potter and my editor, Angelin Adams. Your continued trust drives me to challenge myself and, in turn, to create something meaningful. I feel so lucky to work with an editor of your caliber and expertise. Thank you for letting me fulfill dreams through these journeys. To those working behind the scenes at Clarkson Potter: Stephanie Huntwork, for your art direction and book design. And to Jenny Davis, Bridget Sweet, Kim Tyner, and Darian Keels, your hard work is evident on every page.

Thank you to Nicole Tourtelot, my literary agent—pitching a book that involved global travel at the start of the pandemic was no easy task—and to Anthony DeWitt and Katherine Curkin, I feel so fortunate to work with you both.

To Nino Mottalini, Nepal Asatthawasi, Jeffrey W Miller, Mayer Rus, Hannah Martin, Yumiko Sakuma, Tom Delavan, Pedro Alonso, Chittawadi Chitrabongs, Ishii Hideaki, Alex Tieghi-Walker, Nicky Clennding, Isla van Damme, Sally Mottalini, André Scarpa, Nuno Melo Souza, Michael Tymbios, Francisco Berzunza, Henry Fagan, Helena Fagan, Blair Richardson, Pedro Ferreira, Camron Stone, Maria de Luynes, Enrique Pérez Rosiles, Anna Choe, Haeran Song, Jazmin Hidalgo, Ester Delgado, and Rubén Daza—an enormous thank-you for all of your support.

My next thank-you is to Jay Ireland, who arranged and managed all of our very complex travel for this project. Had you not been involved, this project could never have been so ambitious. You helped navigate three creatives based in three different locations to twelve countries on five continents over the course of a year and during a pandemic—an all but impossible task that you managed with grace and generosity. A big thank-you to you, my friend!

To my parents, thank you again for being part of this journey. You instilled in me at a very young age a love of travel and exploration for which I will forever be grateful.

And, finally, a very special thank-you to my husband, Mike Larocca, and my boys, Wolf and Julian. Mike, thank you for making it so easy to follow my dreams and for being there every part of the journey. And lastly, to Wolf and Julian, it is a privilege to be your mother and watch you grow and explore the world. I hope this book shows you that nature can always be your refuge, and I wish for each of you to find your own adventures in this beautiful world.

High mountains encircle the Engadin Valley in eastern Switzerland.

The author of *Surf Shack* and *Bibliostyle*, **NINA FREUDENBERGER** received her Bachelor of Fine Arts and Bachelor of Architecture from Rhode Island School of Design before launching a career in interior design. She is the founder of the Los Angeles–based interior design firm Freudenberger Design, which specializes in private residential interiors and hospitality projects across the country. In addition, Nina has designed a wide array of home and lifestyle products and collaborations sold nationwide, including rugs, textiles, wallcoverings, and furniture. She currently lives with her husband and two boys in California.